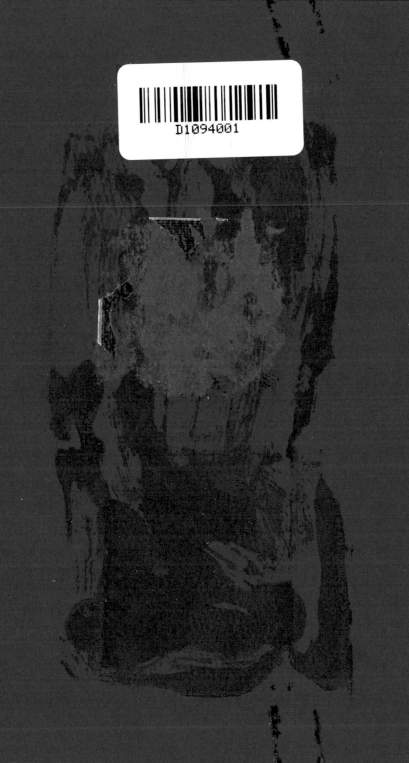

Twayne's English Authors Series

Sylvia E. Bowman, *Editor*

INDIANA UNIVERSITY

Henry Home, Lord Kames

TEAS   82

Henry Home, Lord Kames

By ARTHUR E. McGUINNESS

University of California, Davis

Twayne Publishers, Inc.　:　:　New York

*For
Anne and
Michael*

Preface

Henry Home, Lord Kames, was a Scottish man of letters, who, in his major works at least, made substantial contributions to the history of ideas in the eighteenth century. And, like most of his fellow Scots, he had been more or less forgotten by the literary world. The last several years, however, have witnessed the beginnings of a renewal of interest in eighteenth-century Scottish letters, caused in large measure by an increasing recognition of the accomplishments of the period's literary giant, David Hume. The study of Hume as a literary figure has again made the world aware of the real distinction of the Scottish Enlightenment.

Needless to say, Lord Kames has benefited from this renewed interest in the period. His *Elements of Criticism* has been reprinted after having been out of print for nearly a century. Several articles about his life and works have recently appeared. In addition to the present volume which deals with his accomplishments as a man of letters, at least two other books which will deal with his biography and his culture are being written. In short, after almost two hundred years of neglect, Lord Kames may at last be given the place he deserves in the history of eighteenth-century British literature.

This book will not deal with all of Kames's works. He wrote over a dozen books on subjects ranging from esthetics and psychology to legal history, educational theory, natural history, and farming. He recognized that the eighteenth-century reading public was not monolithic, and his books appealed to a variety of audiences. *Essays on the Principles of Morality and Natural Religion* was a scholarly response to philosophical and theological questions raised by Hume's skepticism. *Introduction to the Art of Thinking* and *Loose Hints upon Education* were intended to be used as handbooks.

I have limited this study of Kames to three of his works—*Essays on the Principles of Morality and Natural Religion, Elements of Criticism,* and *Sketches of the History of Man*—because in these books he focuses on topics essential to the study of eighteenth-century intellectual history. In *Essays* Kames tries to work out some of the conflicts existing between the ethical approaches of the "Moral Sense School" on the one hand, and rationalism and Deism on the other. In developing his argument, he treats such important topics as the nature of sympathy and its role in human communication; the relationship between beauty and virtue; the nature and meaning of justice, freedom, and belief. In *Elements of Criticism* Kames first relates the empirical psychology which he establishes in *Essays* to specifically literary matters and develops a theory of esthetics. The second part of *Elements* concerns itself with such matters of style as versification, figurative language, and the "rules" for composing in the genres of epic and drama. I have limited my discussion of *Sketches of the History of Man* to another matter of theory and practice. The eighteenth century was very concerned with the question of how human development had taken place, whether man had declined from an original state of natural goodness or was originally a savage who had made some progress toward civilization. Kames speculates that neither theory in its extreme form is correct, and he then illustrates his own theory about primitivism and progress by attempting to defend the authenticity of the Ossian poems.

A version of Chapter 6 first appeared as "Lord Kames on the Ossian Poems: Anthropology and Criticism," in *Texas Studies in Literature and Language,* X (Spring, 1968) 65-75. I am grateful to the following for permission to use material under their copyright: the Editorial Committee of the Yale Editions of the Private Papers of James Boswell, Rupert Hart-Davis Limited, Putnam's and Coward-McCann, Schocken Books, and Oxford University Press.

I should like to express my gratitude, first of all, to Professor Ricardo Quintana of the University of Wisconsin, who encouraged me to persevere in this project and who gave me the benefits of his mature insights about the eighteenth century; to Professor Ian Ross of the University of British Columbia and to

Preface

Professor William Lehmann of Syracuse University, who shared their enthusiasm for the Scottish Enlightenment with me and helped me to obtain manuscript material; to Professor Thomas Hanzo of the University of California, Davis, for reading the manuscript and discussing it with me; and to the Committee on Research, University of California, Davis, which supported the project with a Summer Faculty Fellowship and also provided funds which enabled me to have the clerical assistance of Mr. Niklaus Schweizer, Miss Diane Hobe, and Mrs. Nancy Anderson. Finally, I am grateful to my wife, who managed to sublimate her natural antipathy toward the Age of Reason during the entire writing of this book.

ARTHUR E. McGUINNESS
University of California, Davis

Contents

Chronology

1754   *Principles of the Law of Scotland.* Read paper "Of the Laws of Motion" before Edinburgh Philosophical Society.

1755   Involved in a heresy charge before the Assembly, central governing body of the Scottish Church, for positions he took in *Essays.*

1756   *Remarkable Decisions of the Court of Session, 1730–1752.*

1757   *Statute Laws.*

1758   *Historical Law Tracts.*

1759   Home entertains Benjamin Franklin and his son at Kames.

1760   *Principles of Equity.*

1761   *Introduction to the Art of Thinking.*

1762   *Elements of Criticism.*

1763   April 15, Kames appointed Lord Commissioner of Justiciary, the supreme criminal court of Scotland.

1766   *Progress of Flax-husbandry in Scotland.* Kames's wife Agatha inherits estate at Blair-Drummond.

1769   Kames becomes president of the Philosophical Society.

1771   Franklin again the guest of Kames, this time at Blair-Drummond.

1774   *Sketches of the History of Man.*

1775   Boswell begins collecting materials for his projected life of Kames. Has final interview with him just before Kames's death in 1782.

1776   *The Gentleman Farmer.*

1777   *Elucidations respecting the Common and Statute Law of Scotland.*

1780   *Select Decisions of the Court of Session, 1752–1768.*

1781   *Loose Hints upon Education.*

1782   December 21, Kames attends the Court of Session for the last time. December 27, he dies. Buried in Blair Drummond churchyard, Kinkardine, Perthshire.

CHAPTER 1

The Eighteenth-Century Man of Letters

A "conspiracy of silence" has long kept Scottish letters in obscurity. Students learn from histories of British literature that, while Scotland did produce an occasional eccentric genius like Robert Burns, by and large it depended on England for its literary inspiration and its models. Such fixed ideas can remain unchallenged because Scottish literature is generally unavailable to the modern reader. Indeed, most students are introduced to the eighteenth century in courses entitled "The Age of Swift and Pope" and "The Age of Johnson." Such special pleading, which works to the disadvantage of Scottish letters, is especially unfortunate in the latter half of the period when David Hume's literary performance and reputation rivaled that of Samuel Johnson.

Surely eighteenth-century Scottish literature merits consideration in its own right. In addition to Hume, the period produced two distinguished men of letters, James Boswell and Adam Smith; at least three poets, James Thomson, Allan Ramsay, and Robert Burns; two novelists, Tobias Smollett and Henry Mackenzie; at least one notable dramatist, John Home; philosophers like Francis Hutcheson and Thomas Reid; and such critics as George Campbell, Alexander Gerard, Hugh Blair, and Lord Kames.

In the past several years, scholarly interest in the Scottish eighteenth century has increased; and the important literary works of the period are gradually becoming available for the modern reader. Hume's essays have appeared in several inexpensive editions; and the definitive edition of his works, out of print for years, was reprinted in 1965. The important rhetorical treatises of Blair and Campbell are available in new printings. And the Scottish Text Society is making every effort to fill the cultural gap. It is, for example, currently bringing out the poetry of Allan Ramsay; and a new edition of Adam Smith's writings has recently been commissioned and is already being prepared. Perhaps the best indication of renewed interest in the general area of Scottish letters is a new journal, *Studies in Scottish Literature,* which is now in its sixth year of publication.

The study of Lord Kames's life and works serves as an excellent introduction to Edinburgh intellectual life. Kames numbered among his acquaintances every important Scottish literary figure of his day from David Hume to the notorious James Macpherson; he helped to organize one literary society and actively participated in several others. He was at the same time perhaps the best lawyer of his age and a judge in both the civil and criminal supreme courts. His books, as I have indicated in the preface, range from philosophy to farming, and include rhetoric, literary criticism, natural history, law, and education.

One of the most notable literary works to appear in the second half of the eighteenth century was James Boswell's *Life of Samuel Johnson.* It may come as a surprise to some readers to learn that the literary world came close to having another biography by Boswell, this one the life of Lord Kames. Boswell contemplated writing a biography of Kames in 1775 and secured the latter's permission to carry out the project. In that treasure of Boswelliana discovered in the 1920's at Malahide Castle is a portion of the projected life of Kames which Boswell entitled "Materials for Writing the Life of Lord Kames, Taken From His Own Mouth." It covers the period from 1778 to 1782, the year of Kames's death; and it provides, through its record of Kames's reflections over his life, much of the biographical information we have about him.[1]

Lord Kames's early life gave little promise of his later success. Born in 1696 on the family estate at Berwickshire, an area of rolling hills, pleasant streams, and farmlands on the English border, Henry Home—he received the title Lord Kames when he was appointed to the Session Court—was the son of Agnes Walkinshaw Home and George Home. On his father's side he was related to the Earl of Home and on his mother's side to the Walkinshaws of Barrowfield, "whose names are sprinkled throughout the histories and documents of the Rebellion."[2]

As his heritage demanded, Henry was reared a Jacobite and an Episcopalian. And, while he would later shake off the family political commitment and never be scrupulous about religious practice, his religious background meant that he would be "accustomed to the decency and order of the Service Book of the Scottish Episcopalian Church, rather than the violent extempore harangues of the Established Kirk . . . [a fact] not . . . unimportant in shaping the mind of one who was to concern himself so closely with taste and judgment in aesthetic matters."[3]

I *Education and Edinburgh*

Although related to the aristocracy, Henry's father was decidedly a poor relation. Financial considerations prevented Henry from going away to school, so he received his education at home. His biographers delight in telling about his first tutor, John Wingate, whom Boswell describes as "a Nonjurant divine, a Blockhead and a barbarous fellow"[4] from whom young Home learned Latin. Wingate was succeeded by a somewhat gentler tutor who taught Home Greek, mathematics, and natural philosophy.[5] Home did not choose to enter a career in law; the choice was made for him, largely because of his father's impecunity. But, whatever the cause, his education could no longer be continued at home; he had to go up to Edinburgh. Henry left Berwickshire in his late teens; Ian Ross has written well of the sights which greeted him as he approached the Scottish capital:

From a distance, as Gray properly suggests, Edinburgh was and is a noble and striking sight. The Castle breaks the skyline defiantly on its rock, and the tall tenements march down from it to Holyrood Palace, which lies beneath the petrified couchant lion of a hill known as Arthur's Seat. In Henry Home's time the city was encircled by the Flodden Wall; it consisted of two main thoroughfares, the High Street, which connected the Castle with the Palace suburb of the Cannongate, and the Cowgate, which ran in a parallel fashion to the south. A warren of wynds and closes lined these two streets, and from the densely packed houses rose a cloud of smoke which hung over the city, giving it the appropriate title of "Auld Reekie." Midway in the High Street was situated St. Giles, the High Kirk of Edinburgh; to the south of this church lay Parliament Close, a square formed by the buildings at that time given over to the Law Courts.[6]

Edinburgh also had its less pleasing side, as Ross points out a few pages later: "The nasty aspect of Edinburgh in the eighteenth century was chiefly occasioned by the rudimentary nature of the sanitary arrangements, which permitted excrements to be deposited on the streets at certain hours, and made little provision for the removal of that filth or of the refuse from the shops and street markets."[7] As the medieval poet, Dunbar, puts it in his poem "To the Merchants of Edinburgh":

> May nane pass throw your principall gaittes
> For stink of haddockis and scattis,
> For cryis of carlingis and debaittis,
> For fensum flyttingis of defame:
>   Think ye not schame,
> Befoir strangeris of all estaittis
> That sic dishonour hurt your name![8]

Home, who seems to have adjusted to life in the city, began the study of law as an apprentice in the "Writer's Chamber" of John Dickson, a civil lawyer. At about the age of twenty he began the study of civil law with James Craig, Professor of Civil Law at the University of Edinburgh. Home was examined for the bar in 1722 and became an advocate in January, 1723; but he by no means found immediate fortune in the profession. For he told Boswell, "I was ten years at the bar without making ten pounds."[9] In 1732, after the death of his old teacher James Craig, he applied unsuccessfully for the Chair of Roman Law at the University of Edinburgh. In 1736 he helped defend the infamous Captain Porteous; but, more effective in getting his name into influential legal circles were two books, *Remarkable Decisions of the Court of Sessions, 1716–1728* (1728) and *Essays upon several Subjects in Law* (1732). The first was a collection of Scottish legal precedents; the second, a philosophy of law.

Law and culture had a much closer tie in eighteenth-century Edinburgh than they do today. "The law was the prerogative of an educated professional class, a small but influential minority in the country, who were largely responsible for the re-definition of polite culture in eighteenth-century Scotland."[10] Henry Home made a variety of contributions to that culture in addition to his writings. As a member of the Rankenian Club and the Select Society, and as one of the founders of the revived Philosophical Society, he was in constant touch with Edinburgh intellectual life. Speculative problems raised in discussions at the Rankenian Club led to the publication of his first major philosophical work, *Essays on the Principles of Morality and Natural Religion* (1751).

One of the concerns of this club was to improve the use of written English in Scotland. Home was responsible for bringing the distinguished rhetorician Thomas Sheridan to Edinburgh to assist in the project. In the period from 1748 to 1759 he was instrumental in the appointment of three lecturers on rhetoric and *belles-lettres* at the university: Adam Smith, Robert Watson, and Hugh Blair; the latter in 1762 became the first Regius Professor of Rhetoric and Belles-Lettres, a chair which has since been held by some of Britain's most distinguished scholars.

Two anecdotes appear in virtually all biographical essays about Home. Although the stories are probably apocryphal, they do testify to his acerbic public manner, and David Martin's portrait of him in the National Gallery of Scotland has very likely helped give credence to the anecdotes. Ian Ross describes it thus: "His nose appears long, as befits a lawyer; level eyes, the right a little more closed than the left, look quizzically from under full brows and a lofty, lined forehead. High cheekbones and a long jaw, with the skin drawn tightly over them, suggest austerity and combativeness in the face as a whole. It is Kames's mouth, however, which draws one's attention most of all. The overlip is thin, while the underlip is prominent and twists down at the left corner in a cynical and faintly derisive manner."[11] It is said that, while Home was a presiding judge in the Scottish criminal court, an acquaintance of his, who regularly defeated him at chess was tried, convicted of murder, and sentenced to be hanged. After passing sentence, Home is reported to have looked down at him and declared, "Checkmate, Mattie, noo."[12] Home remained on the Scottish bench until a few days before his death in 1782. On leaving his courtroom for the last time, he supposedly turned to the colleagues he had been associated with for the previous thirty years and said, "Fare ye a'weel, ye bitches."

Boswell composed a ballad about Lord Kames in 1766 which lends support to these two anecdotes. In addition to taking swipes at Kames's reputation as a "hanging judge," he has some fun with Kames's penchant for discovering the principles which order all experience and with his tendency to reduce experience to modes of feeling. "Affleck" in the fourth stanza is Boswell's father, Lord Auchinleck, who sat on the same bench with Henry Home.

"Song in the Character of Lord Kames"

1.

Of all the Judges in the land
I surely must be held the Chief;
For none so *cleverly* can hang
A bloody Murderer or Thief.
  Tweedle Tweedle Tweedle Didum
  Up with the Justiciary Court.

2.

With a *sound Critic's* nicest eye
I view the bearing of a Mace;
It's very *Elements* I know
And teach even pompous Brisbane grace.
  Tweedle Tweedle, etc.

3.

And when my own State Trumpet blows
And from the Prison door resounds
I with *intensest Study* make
A *Dictionary*—of the sounds.
  Tweedle Tweedle, etc.

4.

A Trial must not last too long.
The longest life is but a Span,
Affleck may sit for thirty hours,
But I'll *abridge* it when I can.
  Tweedle Tweedle, etc.

5.

For, if a Fellow looks but ill,
His very looks offend me so,
He makes my worst *Emotions* rise,—
So to the gallows let him go.
  Tweedle Tweedle, etc.

6.

And if a Woman is of age
To hang her I'm extremely keen
For 'tis a *Principle* with me
To [hang] all women past fifteen.
  Tweedle Tweedle, etc.

7.

When a poor Pannel's Counsel speak,
Bo!—this will never do at all.
Three days ago I am engag'd
To pass the ev'ning at a Ball.
  Tweedle Tweedle, etc.

8.

And since we mortals here below
Must thro' the *fatal* darkness grope
Develope [we] the mighty ill
To dance in a delusive rope.
  Tweedle Tweedle, etc.

9.

Of all the Judges in the land
I surely must be held the Chief;
For none so *cleverly* can hang
A bloody Murderer or Thief.
  Tweedle, Tweedle, Tweedle Didum
  Up with the Justiciary Court.[13]

We gain a more accurate understanding of Home's personality, however, from considering the men who actively sought him out in the 1750's and 1760's for company as well as for advice. Ian Ross speaks of "élèves" like Adam Smith, William Hamilton of Bangour, James Oswald, and James Forester who gathered around Home.[14] When the young David Hume came to Edinburgh in his teens, he stayed with Home and remained a loyal friend for many years. Because Hume never thought much of his mentor's philosophical position and because Henry Home disapproved of most of David's impetuous publishing ventures, the relationship eventually cooled. But we learn much about the kind of person Home was from letters David Hume wrote to him. The following letter, written in 1737, has a frankness which one would reveal only to his closest friends. Hume's essay on miracles, referred to in the letter and published in 1748, had the very effect on the public which Hume here predicts it would:

DEAR SIR

I am very sorry I am not able to satisfy your Curiosity by giving you some general Notion of the Plan upon which I proceed. But my Opinions are so new, & even some Terms I am oblig'd to make Use of, that I cou'd not propose by any Abridgement to give my System an Air of Likelyhood, or so much as make it intelligible. . . . I have been here near 3 months alwise within a Week of agreeing with Printers, & you may imagine I did not forget the Work itself during that Time, where I began to feel some Passages weaker for the Style & Diction than I cou'd have wisht. The Nearness & Greatness of the Event rouz'd up my Attention, & made me more difficult to please than when I was alone in perfect Tranquillity in France. But here I must tell you one of my Foibles. I have a great Inclination to go down to Scotland this Spring to see my Friends, & have your Advice concerning my philosophical Discoveries; but cannot over-come a certain Shamefacedness I have to appear among you at my Years without having yet a Settlement or so much as having attempted any. How happens it that we Philosophers cannot as heartily despise the world as it despises us? I think in my Conscience the Contempt were as well founded on our Side as on the other.

Having a frankt Letter I was resolv'd to make Use of it, & accordingly enclose some Reasonings concerning Miracles, which I once thought of publishing with the rest, but which I am afraid will give too much Offence even as the World is dispos'd at present. There is Something in the turn of Thought & a good deal in the Turn of Expression, which will not perhaps appear so proper for want of knowing the Context: But the Force of the Argument you'll be judge of as it stands. Tell me your Thoughts of it. Is not the Style too diffuse? Tho as that was a popular Argument I have spread it out much more than the other Parts of the Work. I beg of you show it to no Body, except to Mr. Hamilton, if he pleases; & let me know at your Leizure that you have receiv'd it, read it, & burnt it. I wou'd not even have you make another nameless Use of it, to which it wou'd not be improper, for fear of Accidents.[15]

When Benjamin Franklin journeyed to Scotland from London in 1759, he spent much of his time as a guest at Lord Kames's estate. Helen Randall notes "the high opinion which he formed of Kames as a companion, thinker, and writer," and she points out that Kames was one of only two Scots with whom Franklin corresponded regularly after his visit.[16]

II *Publications and Career*

Home's *Essays,* published in 1751, caused a great stir in Scottish religious and political circles because of his notions about determinism and free will:

... Home argued for necessity and described man's feeling of liberty as at once delusive and God-given for "the uses and conveniences of life." This argument, together with other incidental points, provoked the hostility of the clergy, and the resulting controversy, which lasted for nearly five years, involved three published attacks upon the book, two publications in its defense, the strictures of the Assembly, which removed Home from its commission, and a complaint, brought before the Presbytery of Edinburgh, against the printers and publishers of the *Essays,* to which the respondents, through their counsel, replied at length. The sudden death of the chief opponent, the Rev. George Anderson, brought the affair to a close early in 1756, when the Presbytery dismissed the process. Two years later Home retracted the theory of a delusive feeling of liberty in the second edition of the book, which appeared in 1758. The whole episode was only a tempest in a tea-pot, but throughout he showed the characteristics of tenacity and a fighting spirit with which he is credited in many contemporary accounts. [17]

This controversy aside, *Essays* makes a significant contribution to the debate over the relative value of rationalism, skepticism, and common sense in explaining man's experience of himself, as we shall see in Chapter 2. For Home, common sense, along with sensibility, is the basis of man's moral life; and thus the good man is the man of feeling. Such an approach to morality makes virtue a species of beauty and makes the awareness of both dependent upon taste. Also important in *Essays* is Home's handling of the philosophical problem of the separation of subject and object. Descartes had reasoned that a gap exists between the individual consciousness and the outside world. Home, who refutes Descartes, declares that man is linked to his fellow man by the bond of natural sympathy.

In 1752 Henry Home was elevated to the Sessions Court, the Scottish civil bench, and given the non-hereditary title of Lord Kames, Kames being the name of his family estate. He became a justice in the supreme Scottish Criminal Court in 1763. From all that we know, Lord Kames was a dedicated public servant and did much to stabilize and clarify Scottish law in the years after the political unification of Scotland with England:

> . . . he appeared to his contemporaries to be a learned and capable judge, whose decisions were sound but whose court procedure was more original than conventional. In his printed depositions and judgments he showed the same penchant for analysis which one discovers throughout his more philosophical writings, the same desire to arrive at causes rather than merely to order the facts. He was also known to disregard the established conventions of the court, as is shown in at least two trials where he took occasion to address the jury after the advocates for the defense had summed up their evidence, an innovation which was approved after his death by an act of Parliament.[18]

In 1760 he published his philosophical study of law, *Principles of Equity,* and in 1758 *Historical Law Tracts.* "Kames's point, like that of Montesquieu, was that we can understand the various divisions of law . . . only in the light of their relationship with each other and with the physical environment, economy, customs, religion, temperament of the people who gave rise to the laws."[19]

What impresses us most about Home is his remarkable versatility and the range of his interests. He attacked domestic problems with the same vigor he displayed in public life. He was, for example, "one of the best agriculturalists of his day."[20] The gardens at Blair-Drummond, the estate inherited by his wife Agatha, whom he had married in 1741, provided a pleasant retreat from the hustle and bustle of Edinburgh for many of his friends. Foremost among his agricultural projects was the reclamation of the fifteen-hundred-acre Moss of Kincardine on his estate. The tract was eventually cleared, and "by 1805 seven hundred and twenty people were living there."[21] In 1776 Home wrote *The Gentleman Farmer,* which he described on the title page as "an attempt to improve agriculture by subjecting it to the test of rational principles," a method he had used with such great success in his books on law. Home also published two books on education, *An Introduction to the Art of Thinking* (1761) and *Loose Hints on Education, or, the Culture of the Heart* (1781), as well as a natural history, *Sketches of the History of Man* (1774).

Elements of Criticism, which appeared in 1762, soon became Home's most widely known work. It was generally well received in England, where six editions appeared during Home's lifetime. In Germany, where it appeared in translation less than five years after its English publication, Lessing and Herder both praised it highly.[22] And in America, as Helen Randall points out, *Elements* was a standard rhetoric text until the middle of the nineteenth century. The book was not, however, an unqualified success; David Hume and Adam Smith criticized it, Samuel Johnson thought it "chimerical." In his discussion of the epic, Home made what was to prove a tactical error in pointing out the unnaturalness of modern French epic, the *Henriade.* Unfortunately for Home, the author of the *Henriade* was Voltaire. The latter's predictably acerbic reaction to Home's remarks appeared anonymously in 1764 in the *Gazette littéraire de l'Europe.* Voltaire fixes on the weakest part of *Elements,* where Home tries to establish a mechanical equivalence between the psychological and the physical orders; and, with a nice bit of irony, he professes his admiration for "this Philosopher ... [who] proves to us first of all that we have five senses, and that the impression made sweetly by sounds and colors on our eyes and on our ears is less jarring than a blow on the arm or a knock on the head."[23] Despite the objections of such critics, however, *Elements* had a far greater initial popularity than David Hume's *Treatise of Human Nature*, a book which eventually changed the course of philosophy. Like Home's two books on education, *Elements* offered practical suggestions for the development and improvement of taste to an increasingly curious middle-class.

Lord Kames, who lived to be a very old man, retained his intellectual vigor and wit to the end of his life. *Loose Hints upon Education* was published in 1781, just a year before his death. James Boswell, who was always fascinated by the death of famous men, particularly famous men who had fallen from religious orthodoxy, hovered around the house of the dying David Hume, convinced that the great infidel would experience a religious conversion on his deathbed. Needless to say, Hume did not give him this satisfaction. Boswell was also on hand a few days before the death of Lord Kames, and his notes taken at the time reveal the latter's vitality. Kames, like Hume, had never been devoted to orthodox religious practice; and Boswell was looking for some kind of religious manifestation now that death was approaching. Kames also failed to give him this satisfaction:

(Sunday 22 December 1782.) I called between 3 and 4. Mrs. Drummond said he was weak as yesterday, and in bed, and she desired I would go in and inquire for him. He liked it. I went to his bedside and said, "As I was passing by, I just called to inquire for you, My Lord. I am going to dine with your old freind [*sic*] Lady Dundonald." "Not at that time of day!" said he. "Yes," said I, "It is after three o'clock. How are you, My Lord?" "O, dinna' ask foolish questions. I hope to be better in the evening." "Then in the evening I will have the honour to attend you." I then went and dined and drank tea at Lady Dundonald's, with whom I talked of him, and begged she would give me something to tell that would divert him. She did so. I called again on him and was shewn to his bedside. "How are you now, My Lord?" He recollected clearly his having desired I would not ask him, and catching me at it again, he said, "Have you been debauching with Lady Dundonald?" "No," said I, and immediately gave him *un précis,* as the french say, of what had passed.... (This tickled his fancy. He put out his cold right hand and chucked me under the chin, as if he had said, "You're a Wag.") ... He did not speak to me any more. He lay with the same countenance which he has had for several years, though somewhat emaciated; and while I looked at him, I could not help wondering why he did not answer me as usual. To perceive Lord Kames, who used to be all alive, now quite quiescent, was a change to which my mind could not easily agree. I told him that I had heard Dr. Blair preach this afternoon to a very crowded Audience, Lady Derby being in Church, and that he gave us an excellent sermon on our years being as a tale that is told. I sat a little longer by him. He twice put out his hand and took mine cordially. I regretted that he did not say one word as a dying man. Nothing edifying, nothing pious. His Lady told me he had not said a word to her of what he thought of himself at present. I sat a long time with her. Mr. Sandilands, his agent, came. And soon after, My Lord to my surprise was supported into the room and sat down on a Settee. But he did not speak and seemed to be very uneasy, so in a few moments he made a sign to his servant and was led away. I came home.[24]

It is unfortunate that Boswell never completed his projected life of Lord Kames. Had he done so, Kames would most certainly have retained the literary reputation he had in the eighteenth century. The forthcoming publication of the Malahide Castle papers in popular form, along with the several studies of Kames now being done, may perhaps restore to him some measure of that reputation. This book will help to show that he deserves it.

CHAPTER 2

Essays on the Principles of Morality and Natural Religion

ESSAYS on the Principles of Morality and Natural Religion (1751), Lord Kames's first major belletristic work, contains the kinds of paradox which Maynard Mack identifies with the uniquely eighteenth-century quality of "tension." A concise exposition of the moral and social theories which Kames would continue to work on for the rest of his life, the book attempts to work out a compromise between philosophical and theological extremes which had split the Augustan world—rationalistic religion (or Deism), intuitionism, psychological egoism, and altruism.

I Rationalism and Skepticism

The complex of ideas which forms the intellectual history of the seventeenth and eighteenth centuries can without excessive oversimplification be reduced to three major movements: rationalism, skepticism, and common sense. And, if we add some term like "tradition" to the beginning of the series, we have what is in effect the full circle of challenge and reaction which emerged during the Enlightenment. Rationalism challenged the unphilosophical nature of man's traditional assumptions; skepticism confronted the timid logic of rationalism; common sense attempted to salvage what was left of tradition from the spiritual desert where skepticism had left it. Of course, no period in the history of ideas develops with such clear-cut divisions. Actually all four of these general ideas continued throughout the eighteenth century, often in combination with one another as intellect and, occasionally, prudence demanded.

To understand what Lord Kames was trying to accomplish in *Essays*, we must first take a closer look at two of these general ideas—rationalism and skepticism. The seeds of both these philosophical movements, as Leslie Stephen has pointed out, were sown by Descartes (1596-1650), whose major work, *Discourse on Method*, appeared in 1637. One of Descartes's principal targets in this work was tradition and the intellectually moribund complacence which it encouraged. His insistence on an experimental verification for all philosophical principles challenged a complacent scholasticism which had reduced the philosophy of St. Thomas Aquinas to a deductive system founded on non-empirical a priori assertions. Descartes's new experimental approach emphasized the danger of basing an explanation of man's nature on such an untrustworthy foundation.

Descartes's epistemological method was, of course, to subject every proposition to what he called "methodical doubt" in order to insure that only those propositions certainly true were accepted. A proposition is true, according to Descartes, if we cannot contradict it without involving ourselves in a logical absurdity. Descartes finally arrives at several such "true" propositions, the most important of which is the reality of man's intellectual experience. Intellectual activity assures the thinker of his own existence and illustrates Descartes's famous principle, "I think, therefore I am." Through a similar direct inspection of his own experience, Descartes arrives at several other certain propositions, among them the reality of matter and the existence of God. The Cartesian system develops from absolute certitude about these three fundamental realities—mind, matter, and God.

At first it might appear odd that the demise of reason is attributed to a writer so devoted to its defense, but a closer look at the implications of Descartes's philosophy should make this attribution clear. Descartes supposedly rejected a philosophical system constructed on a priori principles, but his own philosophy contains similar principles. If the test for the certitude of a proposition is the logical impossibility of its contradictory, later philosophers would point out that there is nothing intrinsically illogical about the contradictories of each of Descartes's three fundamental propositions. It is quite possible to doubt the existence of mind or personal identity, to doubt the existence of matter, and to doubt the existence of God. The ultimate logic of Descartes's method, in other words, produces complete skepticism.

Before considering these developments toward skepticism, we should understand an important quality of Enlightenment thought which A. O. Lovejoy has called "uniformitarianism": "This is the first and fundamental principle of this general and pervasive philosophy of the Enlightenment. The reason, it is assumed to be evident, is identical in all men; and the life of reason therefore, it is tacitly or explicitly inferred, must admit of no diversity."[1] What a man induces from an examination of his own consciousness, whether it be skepticism, rationalism, or intuitionalism, he can confidently assert to be true for all men. Paradoxically, then, the supposedly scientific, psychological method of empiricism is limited to the consciousness of a single subject. Lord Kames proceeds on the same assumption in *Essays*. When he speaks of the moral sentiments of man, he actually means those which he is conscious of in himself and which he then predicates of man in general. Descartes likewise assumed that his conclusions about man's ability to know had a universal validity.

Depending on the particular bias of the commentator, Descartes is either praised or damned for having recognized or created the metaphysical gulf between subject and object. Following his system, as it has been briefly described above, the two ineluctable realities of human experience are mind and matter, each with characteristics so unique and mutually exclusive that there can be no contact between them:

What is our self? It is the single, indivisible, and therefore indestructible unit, which we call the soul, and from the very mode of proof it is evident that the essence of the soul is thought. Knowing the nature of the soul by direct intuition, we also know the nature of its necessary opposite—matter. For matter must be that which does not think, and, further, must be that abstraction which exists under all the varying forms of the visible world. Matter, that is, becomes almost identical with space. Its essence is extension, though we may perhaps throw in the quality of impenetrability, just, as we may say, to stiffen it into the necessary consistency....

Here then we have our realities. The antithesis between subject and object is represented by the two absolute substances—the soul and matter; whilst God, the eternal and self-existent substance, sustains and regulates their relations. And now, having the necessary starting-point, we might proceed to deduce the world from our ideas, in full security that the ideas must correspond to facts. But here, unluckily, occurs the great difficulty which perplexed Descartes and his followers. What is the soul? It is the opposite of matter, and utterly devoid of all material qualities. And what is matter? It is the opposite of the soul, and by no alteration or manipulation can thought be got out of it. If so, how are we to bridge over the gulf between two contradictories? How are we to conceive of any reciprocal action between the two or of one upon the other?[2]

An important part of the history of ideas between Descartes and Kames involves various attempts either to pursue the logical implications of the Cartesian dichotomy or to restore somehow the basis for contact between man's mind and the world.

In the second part of *Essays*, Lord Kames addresses himself to such metaphysical questions as the authority of the senses, the nature of causation, and the existence of God. All three of these had been undermined by skepticism which was the logical development of Descarte's methodic doubt. John Locke, Bishop Berkeley, and David Hume are the foremost British exponents of skeptical philosophy. Locke (1632-1704) considered himself a defender of Christianity against the evils of skepticism and his book, *The Reasonableness of Christianity* (1695), would seem to put him in the rationalist camp. In his most important philosophical work, *Essay Concerning Human Understanding* (1690), however, he takes positions favorable to skepticism.

An avowed empiricist, Locke recognized certain weaknesses in the Cartesian system, especially in its handling of matter. Our experience with objects, Locke noted, gives us no direct experience of what philosophers have called "substance," that metaphysical principle which accounts for the unity of an object and in which all accidents inhere. What we actually experience are certain "primary qualities" which really belong to the object and certain "secondary qualities," like color, which do not really belong to the object at all but exist in the eye of the beholder. Locke does not deny the existence of substance, but he questions whether man can directly experience it. He is more orthodox in his handling of two other major concerns of eighteenth-century speculative thought—personal identity and causation. Locke's theories about ideas and imagination are also extremely important, but they relate more directly to a theory of the beautiful which will be discussed in more detail in later chapters on *Elements of Criticism*.

Bishop George Berkeley (1685-1753) and David Hume (1711-76) developed an extreme form of skepticism which Kames challenges in *Essays*. Berkeley, in an attempt to defend the spiritual side of human nature, answered the materialists by questioning the existence of matter. All man can know with certainty, he maintained, is his own subjective existence. What one assumes to be external objects are really sense impressions. Whether these derive from a material source external to the subject, whether they come from divine intervention, or whether they are figments of one's own imagination can never be persuasively demonstrated.

While Berkeley effectively questioned the existence of matter, Hume questioned the existence of mind, of personal identity, and of causation. An unrelenting examination of our own experience, according to Hume, reveals only discrete sense impressions. Custom and habit have perhaps convinced man that these impressions have their source in an object external to himself, that his mind is a power independent of experience which organizes and controls these impressions, and that he himself remains essentially the same person through his entire life; but none of this can be philosophically demonstrated. Nor can it be demonstrated that one object has the power to produce some change in another object. The notion of causality is as unphilosophical as the notion of mind and matter.

It should be pointed out that neither Berkeley nor Hume insisted that their philosophy be lived. Both recognized that, outside the study, a man must perforce accept the conventions of mind and matter. The important thing is that this recognition was practical rather than philosophical. Acceptance does not involve demonstration. In a curious way, therefore, both of these skeptical philosophers also relate to what later came to be known as the Common-Sense movement, one which insisted that all knowledge derives from certain a priori principles which no reasonable man can deny. What Thomas Reid would call "truth," David Hume called "custom." Lord Kames's attempts to answer the skeptics also depends on this commonsense approach.

While skepticism and empiricism characterize the speculations of those writers who are considered today as most important in the intellectual history of the Enlightenment, a more historical point of view reveals something quite different. A few great thinkers may have been skeptics, but by and large this late-seventeenth and early eighteenth-century period can fairly be called "the Age of Reason." Perhaps the quality which most accurately describes the period is "optimism"; for it was an age "when men believed that the important truths had been discovered or were rapidly being discovered, that such truths would be acknowledged by universal consent, and that there was nothing more but to enjoy the fruits of this happy state of intellectual contentment. The word *reason* had not 'lost its unequivocal simplicity,' and there was confidence in the 'synthesis of the "positive" and the "rational." ' "[3] Rationalism, in other words, provided a respectable and persuasive answer to the first rumblings of the new philosophy.

Two kinds of rationalism appear in this period, both of them important in Kames's works. One of these can be called "intuitive", the other, "discursive."[4] Intuitive rationalism conceives of the reason as an almost Kantian faculty which can grasp a priori first principles. "Reason" in this sense becomes "feeling" in the eighteenth century and underlies the school of moral sentiments or the Common-Sense school. Discursive rationalism, on the other hand, proceeds on the dangerous premise that argument is the only source of truth and on a premise which sounds a good deal like Descartes: if a principle cannot be demonstrated rationally, it is not true. This form of rationalism developed out of a desire, particularly on the part of Anglican divines, to meet the challenges which the new philosophy of empiricism posed for religious orthodoxy.

Speculative theology, which rejected such orthodox guaranties of truth as authority and revelation, and relied instead for certitude on the operation of discursive reason, was most commonly called "Deism." For the Deists, natural religion, that is, those truths which reason could arrive at independently, took the place of revealed religion. The titles of some of their books indicate the direction of their thought: *The Reasonableness of Christianity, Christianity Not Mysterious, Principles and Connections of Natural and Revealed Religion*. We might add the title of Kames's book, *Essays on the Principles of Morality and Natural Religion*, with emphasis on the final phrase. Leslie Stephen summarizes the position of one of the most distinguished Deists, Matthew Tindal:

The unassisted reason of man is abundantly able to discover the few and simple truths of which genuine religion consists. The argument of the Churches is dexterously inverted. Man, they urged, cannot by his own powers discover the mysteries of revelation; therefore he must bow to the authority of those to whom God has confided the only key to the truth. Man, retorted Tindal, cannot discover your mysteries; but God must have dealt equally with all men; and, therefore, doctrines not revealed to all cannot be doctrines imposed upon all by God; reason, the only faculty granted to all men, must of necessity be sufficient to guide all men to truth. Reason is of necessity the sole judge.[5]

Contemplation of man and of the universe revealed a structure minutely ordered and harmonized by the impersonal creator who originally set it in motion. The order of man and human society is a microcosmic reflection of that in the universe.

Such hubristic reliance on man's rational faculty as a guide to truth represented a grave danger to faith. And yet it is not much of an exaggeration to say that most serious speculative theology in the Enlightenment adopted the Deistic method although it might not always agree with the conclusions of the Deists. Even Samuel Clarke, who proposed to defend Christianity, referred to himself as a Christian Deist. When the nature, and indeed the very existence, of reason began to be challenged by the new philosophy, discursive rationalism had nothing but its a priori principles, quite unconvincing at best, with which to meet the attack. Obviously, with the matter of faith at stake, some answer to the skeptics other than rationalism had to be devised. The answer, which Kames incorporates into *Essays*, grows out of the neo-Platonic tradition of the seventeenth century, but it is also combined with a peculiarly Scottish form of empiricism. It is generally called the theory of "moral sentiments."

II *The "Moral Sense" School*

To return for a moment to a distinction made above, many writers important in seventeenth- and eighteenth-century intellectual history were concerned with two problems—man's nature and his conduct. Most considered both problems, since one follows so logically from the other. For the discursive rationalists, moral philosophy offered no problems, since the principles for human conduct need have no relation to actual human experience. For skeptics like Hume, moral philosophy involved living rather than speculation, and therefore we find much less logical intrepidity in Hume's essay on morals than in his essay on human understanding. In a very important way moral philosophy during the eighteenth century began to take precedence over epistemology as the defenses of discursive rationalism crumpled before skepticism. An analysis of how man should act could provide a more acceptable explanation of what man is. It is no accident that, while morality is the final subject in Hume's *Treatise*, it is the first subject of Kames's *Essays*. And the moral philosophy which developed in the eighteenth century was not discursive but grew out of another more neo-Platonic kind of rationalism which became identified in the eighteenth century with "intuition."

Two schools of moral philosophy emerged in England in the seventeenth and early eighteenth centuries that were inspired by the writings of Thomas Hobbes and Lord Shaftesbury. According to Hobbes and his most notable eighteenth-century disciple, Mandeville, man acts solely from a motive of selfishness or self-love. For Shaftesbury and for men like Francis Hutcheson, who were profoundly influenced by Shaftesbury, man is essentially good; his motives are selflessness and benevolence. Lord Kames in *Essays* acknowledges the contribution of Hobbes and Shaftesbury to the history of moral philosophy and tries to work out a compromise between psychological egoism and altruism. More important than the extreme and mutually exclusive conclusions of these writers, however, is their similar observation about human nature. Man, they said, is not motivated by reason; he is motivated by feeling. If reason plays any role in human action, it must be considered part of man's affective consciousness.

Shaftesbury's most notable contribution to Kames's system of morality is his theory of internal sense, one which was later refined by Kame's fellow Scot, Francis Hutcheson. Shaftsbury, revealing his heritage in the neo-Platonism of the late seventeenth century with its doctrine of innate ideas, proposes that human knowledge is not achieved solely through the five external senses. Man also has an innate awareness of good and evil which Shaftesbury calls his 'internal sense" or his "moral sense." True enough, the operation of the moral sense depends upon experience—and here Shaftesbury parts company with the neo-Platonists—but the moral sense is common to all men; and all men therefore have potentially the same feelings about good and evil. Here again is the naïveté of uniformitarianism. Shaftesbury's direct inspection of his own consciousness convinces him about the psychology of human nature.

The doctrine of the moral sense had enormous influence on eighteenth-century thought. In a way, the moral sense is no different from that much-maligned Augustan cliché, common sense. Both imply that man somehow has intuitive knowledge which cannot be demonstrated, but which, nevertheless, is quite real. This kind of dogmatic anti-intellectualism, another quality that Lovejoy finds paradoxically characteristic of the English Enlightenment,[6] is the only reply the age offers to the questions of David Hume until the later appearance of Immanuel Kant.

For Shaftesbury—as for Hutcheson, Kames, and a host of other Scottish and English writers—the moral sense is intimately related to the sense of beauty; and moral philosophy thus becomes extremely important in esthetics, as we shall see in the next chapter. Shaftesbury, in fact, considers the moral sense and the esthetic sense to be two manifestations of the same principle of human nature, essentially a response to the order and purposefulness of creation. What is good is what is beautiful. Although Kames, like Hutcheson, distinguishes several internal senses to explain the various experiences of man's affective consciousness, he nevertheless retains Shaftesbury's idea of the intimate connection between beauty and virtue.

Turning now to Lord Kames's *Essays on the Principles of Morality and Natural Religion,* we should have some idea about how the book fits into eighteenth-century intellectual history.

We should not be surprised at such odd combinations as anti-rationalism and empiricism, natural theology and moral sentiments, freedom and necessity. If the strongest impression we have of Kames's thought is that it is paradoxical, we have responded to a central truth not only about Kames, but about most serious thinkers of the English eighteenth century.

III *Sympathy and Human Relations*

Essays on the Principles of Morality and Natural Religion is divided into two parts. In Part I, Kames defines the natural law, its foundation in human emotions, and its manifestation in such internal senses as the moral sense, the esthetic sense, duty, and justice. Part II combines epistemology, ontology, cosmology, and natural theology in an attempt to defend from the attacks of the skeptics the idea of self, the authority of the senses, causality, and the existence of God. As Ian Ross has pointed out, the common-sense view of man which Kames works out in *Essays* informs such later works as *Elements of Criticism, Historical Law Tracts,* and *Sketches of the History of Man.*[7] In the last work, Kames considers many of the same ideas about morality and natural religion once again; and on certain issues, such as liberty and necessity, he revises his position. Those sections of *Sketches* relevant to Kame's moral philosophy are considered in this chapter, although that work is the subject of later chapters devoted to Kames's ideas about the evolution of culture.

In the Advertisement to *Essays* Lord Kames describes the plan of the book essentially in the terms we have outlined, and he notes his intention "to prepare the way, for a proof of the existence and perfections of the Deity, which is the chief aim in this undertaking."[8] Significantly, Kames conceives of this kind of natural theology in terms which suggest intuitive rationalism and sensibility. Thus proof does not necessarily mean demonstration; it more often means the analysis of human feeling. He declares, ". . . our reasonings on some of the most important subjects, rest ultimately upon sense of feeling" (i).

Kames's purpose in his first essay, "Of Our Attachment to Objects of Distress," is to give the reader a dramatic example of man's feelings. Beginning with simple feelings, he works toward the more complex feelings involved in man's knowledge of God.

In this essay Kames makes two points central to his moral philosophy and later to his esthetic theory: first, the inadequacy of such reductions as self-love to explain human action; second, the nature and importance of sympathy. One of the curiosities of human experience is that man is not only drawn to such objects of distress as executions and burning houses, but that he somehow finds these distressful situations pleasing. Abbé Dubos had attempted to explain the paradox through a principle of activity: inactivity is man's greatest burden; and any action, not matter how distasteful, pleases more than inactivity. Kames points out that, if this were the case, only idlers would be found at such spectacles as executions. By distinguishing the experience of the external senses into complex impressions which include an initial impression, a reaction of pleasure or pain, and a feeling of desire or aversion, and then by illustrating how that which is pleasurable does not always produce desire, nor that which is painful aversion, Kames refutes, to his own satisfaction at least, Dubos's claim that man is motivated to action by pleasure or pain. Self-love, in other words, is not the sole motive for action as Dubos, as well as Locke and Hume, had claimed.

In back of such a paradox as our attachment to objects of distress, Kames goes on, lies the principle of sympathy. Sympathy, as the term occurs in *Essays* and again in *Elements of Criticism*, has two meanings. It can mean (and, in fact, almost always does mean in *Essays*) something like pity: sorrow for someone distressed or unhappy arising from an understanding of his emotional experience. In *Elements of Criticism* the term signifies man's ability to participate in the emotional experience of another and to re-create the same emotional experience in himself. Sympathy in this second sense informs Kames's theory of artistic communication.

In *Essays*, however, Kames describes sympathy as a motive for human action that is at least as influential as self-love: ". . . nature, which designed us for society, has connected us strongly together, by a participation of the joys and miseries of our fellow creatures. We have a strong sympathy with them; we partake of their afflictions; we grieve with them and for them; and, in many instances, their misfortunes affect us equally with our

[38]

own" (16). Note how assuredly Kames speaks about a principle which he makes no attempt to explain. Here is the uniformitarianism of common sense: what is true for oneself is at least potentially true for all men.

Philosophical certitude aside, Kames's ideas about sympathy reveal an awareness of what Martin Buber calls in the twentieth century the "I-Thou" relationship. Sympathy provides the bridge between man and man, or between subject and object—the bridge which Descartes despaired of ever finding; and it enables man to escape from loneliness. Western thought would have to wait for Kant to work out a philosophical structure for this experience, but Kames and the common-sense school certainly were aware of man as a social being:

Nor ought we to judge of this principle, as any way vitious or faulty: for besides, that it is the great cement of human society, we ought to consider, that, as no state is exempt from misfortunes, mutual sympathy must greatly promote the security and happiness of mankind. And 'tis a much more comfortable situation, that the prosperity and preservation of each individual should be the care of the whole species, than that every man, as the single inhabitant of a desert island, should be left to stand or fall by himself, without prospect of regard, or assistance from others. (16–17)

The operation of sympathy enables man to share in the emotional experience of others, but it also produces pleasure. What should revolt actually attracts, a phenomenon of human psychology which Kames observes but makes no attempt to explain: "Far from having any aversion to pain, occasioned by the social principles, we reflect upon such pain with satisfaction, and are willing to submit to it upon all occasions with chearfulness and heart-liking, just as much as if it were a real pleasure" (26). Such a combination of sympathy and attraction also answers, to Kames's satisfaction, a problem which has long intrigued literary critics—the pleasure of tragedy. Tragic pleasure is not, as Dubos had insisted, a rejoicing in the fact that we are not the unfortunate hero. In *Elements of Criticism* Kames works out more fully a theory he merely suggests here: the human mind does not distinguish between real and fictitious objects. Thus drama can engage the social passions as intensely as life. Artistic selection and arrangement can, in fact, make fiction more moving than fact:

> Tragedy is an imitation or representation of human characters and actions. 'Tis a feigned history which generally makes a stronger impression, than what is real; because, if it be a work of genius, incidents will be chosen to make the deepest impressions, and will be so conducted, as to keep the mind in continual suspense and agitation, beyond what commonly happens in real life. By a well wrought tragedy, all the social passions are roused. The first scene is scarce ended before we are engaged. We take a sudden affection to some of the personages represented. We come to be attached to them as to our bosom-friends, and hope and fear for them, as if the whole were a true history, instead of a fable. (18–19)

A drama however, and for that matter any artistic performance, becomes a "work of genius" which makes the "deepest impressions" only when it possesses that quality of realism which Kames calls "ideal presence." It becomes the artist's responsibility to create the illusion of reality if he wishes his audience to respond sympathetically.

IV *Beauty and Virtue*

Having established sympathy as a motive of human action, Kames now turns to human action in general and works out a theory of natural law. This second essay of Part I, "Of the Foundation and Principles of the Law of Nature," is divided into nine chapters: "Of the Foundation of the Law of Nature," "Of the Moral Sense," "Of Duty and Obligation," "Of the Different Orders of Moral Beauty," "Of the Principle of Action," "Of the Source of the Laws of Nature According to Some Authors," "Of Justice and Injustice," "Of the Primary Laws of Nature," and "Of the Laws of Nature." In the introduction to the essay, Kames opposes systems of moral philosophy based on an unrealistic reduction, which either considers man an angelic creature as Shaftesbury and other neo-Pelagians had done, or considers him a brute animal, as did Hobbes. Kames proposes to base his moral system on "facts and experiments"; and, in doing so, he reveals that curious combination of "moral Newtonianism"[9] and reliance on a priori propositions that is so characteristic of the Common-Sense school. Experiment, of course, need not proceed beyond the consciousness of the experimenter.

Kames begins his supposedly empirical investigation of natural law by distinguishing three propositions which underlie it, at least two of which are gratuitously assumed: first, the connection between a being and its actions (cause and effect); second, the common nature of certain creatures based on an observation of their actions; and third, the goodness of all actions conforming to this common nature, and the evil of those which fail to conform to it.

Shaftesbury and Hutcheson emphasize the fact that beauty has an intimate connection with virtue. Both are feelings rather than qualities in objects or kinds of intellectual assent. The pleasure or pain caused by sense perception determines the esthetic and moral character of the object or action perceived. Kames develops these notions in Chapter III, "Of the Moral Sense," and thus involves himself in a debate over the nature of beauty which had begun with Locke's observations about the primary and secondary qualities of perceived objects. Like Kames, most eighteenth-century critics tended to consider beauty an emotion rather than a judgment. Man's emotional response to sense impressions has a complexity similar to impressions themselves. Initial pleasure in an object that simply exists can be followed by a more intense pleasure in perceiving an object that is directed toward some end. Two ideas central to Kames's critical theory emerge here for the first time: the importance of purpose or final cause in the esthetic experience, and the levels of esthetic awareness.

The second idea belongs to the development of taste, manners, and morals which Kames works out more fully in *Elements of Criticism* and in *Sketches of the History of Man*. Like sympathy, the feeling of beauty can be evoked by either natural or artificial objects and actions. Beauty is more usually associated with the experience of a work of art than sympathy, only because in an artistic creation the purposefulness is more immediately apparent: "... the term [approbation] is justly applied to works of art, because it means more than being pleased with such an object merely as existing. It imports a peculiar beauty, which is perceived upon considering the object as fitted to the use intended" (45). It appears from this quotation that Kames considers beauty as a utilitarian would, but we must remember that Kames consistently identifies "use" with final causality; consequently, his position is no more utilitarian than that of the scholastics.

Kames then establishes a relation between beauty and morality. He points out the similarities between the two in Chapter III and emphasizes the important differences in Chapter IV. If the more refined kind of beauty is either a response to final causality, that is, to the relation of object and action to end, or a response to action fitted to object—then we may describe fitting or suitable human action as potentially beautiful. Beauty in this sense becomes moral beauty. And, since every affective response must proceed from some faculty, according to Kames, this feeling proceeds from what he calls the moral sense: "This peculiar feeling, or modification of beauty and deformity in human actions, is known by the name of *moral beauty*, and *moral deformity*. In it consists the *morality* and *immorality* of human actions; and the power or faculty, by which we perceive this difference among actions, passes under the name of the *moral sense*" (50).

Is the moral sense nothing more than a faculty which accounts for our response to the fittingness or unfittingness of human action? Shaftesbury and Hutcheson had indicated this in their earlier speculations, and seemingly Kames has come to a similar conclusion. In Chapter V, however, Kames considers "duty and obligation" and reveals how his moral philosophy avoids the unrealistic extremism of both of his predecessors. As has been noted several times, Lord Kames may not have a remarkably original mind, but he does possess the ability to work out a balanced or common-sense position which accurately reflects his age. In the case of the moral sense, he refuses to be bound by the limitations of the Shaftesburian system and understands its hedonistic implications. Direct inspection of his own experience reveals a distinction between morality and beauty. Response to or contemplation of human action includes a feeling of right and wrong which accompanies the feeling of fittingness or unfittingness. This instinctive feeling of right and wrong, Kames declares, produces all of man's notions of "duty, obligation, ought, and should." No moral philosophy before him, he affirms, has sufficiently clarified this extremely important distinction between "fit" and "right." Both the sense of beauty and the moral sense respond to "fitness"; only the moral sense responds to "rightness."

As has been explained, the moral sense seems to include rational elements such as reflection and judgment, since these are usually involved in terms like "fitness" and "virtue." Kames, however, strongly objects to the suggestion that reason plays any part in determining virtuous action, and he criticizes such suggestions in the work of two of his most eminent contemporaries, Joseph Butler and Samuel Clarke. While generally approving of Butler's work, Kames felt it necessary to make clear that conscience, or the moral sense, is a feeling which precedes reflection: "It proceeds from a direct feeling, which we have upon presenting the object, without the intervention of any sort of reflection." Moral sense "is the voice of God within us which commands our strictest obedience, just as much as when his will is declared by express revelation" (63-64). In Chapter VI Kames defends antirationalism even more strongly in objecting to Clarke's rationalistic moral philosophy. Clarke, according to Kames, has attempted to put reason in the place of feeling: " ... the Author of nature has not left our actions to be directed by so weak a principle as reason: and a weak principle it must be to the bulk of mankind, who have little capacity to enter into abstract reasoning; whatever effect it may have upon the learned and contemplative" (98–99) .

Definition of the moral sense gives us only half of a moral philosophy. Kames devotes Chapter V, "Of the Principles of Action," and Chapter VIII, "Of the Primary Laws of Nature," to an investigation of what motivates human action. In these chapters Kames states his clearest objections to moral philosophies which reduce human action to the operation of a single principle whether that principle be psychological egoism or altruism. For Kames, human activity is a complex business and proceeds from a variety of motives. Reductionism leads inevitably to argument, never to truth:

... it is lamentable to find the world divided about these primary laws, almost as much as they commonly are about the most airy and abstract points. Some authors acknowledge no principle in man, but what is altogether selfish; and it is curious to observe how they wrest and torture every social principle, to give it the appearance of selfishness. Others exalt human nature much above its just standard, give no quarter to selfishness, but consider man as bound to direct every action to the good of the whole, and not to prefer his own interest to that of others. (120–21)

Such attempts to simplify experience reveal a lack of careful induction: "'Men of narrow minds and contracted principles, naturally fall in with the selfish system. The system of universal benevolence attracts the generous and warm-hearted" (122).

Kames arranges this variety of motives for human actions into appetites, passions, and affections. His complete explanation of human conduct, therefore, includes these principles of action and "the moral sense, by which these principles are governed and directed" (77). He was, apparently, unaware of the contradiction between his objection to other categorical systems and his own system, which is equally categorical. Thus, while he objects to proposing selfishness or benevolence as the sole motive for human conduct, he does not hesitate to propose his own motives, perhaps because instead of one there are five: self-preservation, self-love, fidelity, gratitude, and benevolence. Again the sole guarantee for truth that there are five principles of action, no more and no less, is Kames's personal experience.

V *Justice and the Origin of Man*

Essays is most often described as an unsuccessful attempt to refute the philosophy of David Hume. This generalization is inaccurate for two reasons: first, the book is more clearly a systematic statement of Kames's own moral philosophy; second, Hume's philosophy has a common-sense dimension much like that of Kames particularly in the treatment of the passions and of morals. Nevertheless, Kames does take issue with Hume at several points in Part I, and quite regularly in Part II. In Chapter VIII of the second essay, Kames attempts to refute Hume's theory that justice is not a natural virtue but an artificial one which society adopts for the common good. Property rights, by the same reasoning, derive from an artificial convention.

Kames answers Hume with an argument from his version of natural law—man has the natural right to anything he requires to satisfy his natural instincts. In this case, since man is required by nature to labor, property must be his natural right. "... when self-preservation, the most eminent of our principles of action, directs every individual to labour for himself in the first place; man, without a sense or feeling of property, would be an absurd being" (106). That justice is a natural virtue follows from man's natural right to property. The violation of another's property rights makes man feel that he has committed an act of injustice.

Kames concludes Essay II with a chapter about the origin of man, the relation between reflection and taste, and the order of the universe. The problem of man's origin, or the original condition of man, had intrigued Englishmen since Hobbes had challenged orthodox ideas about the state of innocence and original sin. According to Hobbes—and later Hume—man was originally a brutish and completely selfish creature. Society emerged as the least objectionable means of controlling his naturally anarchic tendencies.

Kames objects to the implications of such a theory of natural history: "Brutish manners imply brutish principles of action; and, from this view of the original state of mankind, it may seem that moral virtues are not natural, but acquired by means of education and example in a well-regulated society. In a word, that the whole moral part of our system is artificial, as justice is represented by a late writer" (136-37). The "late writer" is, of course, Hume. Kames does not really answer these objections; he merely relies on common sense. If an inspection of human conduct now reveals principles of action natural to man, then primitive man must have possessed them. His savage conduct means only that his innate moral sense had not yet been sufficiently exercised. In these early days man followed an easier path of conduct and was not aware of the more refined moral principles.

For Kames, therefore, moral conduct directly relates to manners; both are capable of improvement or refinement; the virtuous man becomes, therefore, the man of feeling or the man of taste. If we accept Kames's premise that human action is prompted and controlled by feeling, the equation of refined sensibility and virtue follows logically. It is not an oversimplification to say that, for Kames, natural history records the development of taste:

The contemplation is beautiful, when we compare our gradual improvement in knowledge and in morality. We begin with surveying particular objects, and lay in a stock of simple ideas. Our affections keep pace, being all directed to particular objects; and, during this period, we are governed principally by our passions and appetites. So soon as we begin to form complex and general ideas, these also become the objects of our affections. Then it is, that love to our country begins to exert itself, benevolence to our neighbours and acquaintances, affection to our relations as such. We acquire by degrees the taste of public good, and of being useful in life. The pleasures of society thicken [*sic*] upon us. The selfish passions are tamed and subdued, and the social affections gain the ascendant. ... [The moral sense] improves gradually like our other powers and faculties, 'till it comes to be productive of the strongest as well as most delicate feelings. To clear this point, everyone must be sensible of the great advantages of education and imitation. The most polished nations differ only from savages in refinement of taste, which, being productive of nice and delicate feelings, is the source of pleasure and pain, more exquisite than savages are susceptible of. Hence it is, that many actions, which make little impression upon savages, appear to us elegant and beautiful. (142–44)

This principle becomes very important in Kames's theory of criticism, for the best critic possesses the most refined sensibility. Art consists of a structure of feelings rather than a logical arrangement of topics.

In his theory of moral revolution, Kames emphasizes what could be called a Deistic view of order in man and, by implication, in the universe: "Man is a complex machine, composed of various principles of motion, which may be conceived as so many springs and weights, counteracting and balancing one another. These being accurately adjusted, the movement of life is beautiful, because regular and uniform. But if some springs or weights be withdrawn, those which remain, acting now without opposition from their antagonist forces, will disorder the balance, and derange the whole machine" (140–41). This mechanical metaphor, which appears at several points in *Essays,* suggests how very close to materialism were those who struck out against it. Surely passages like this encouraged the National Assembly's suspicions about Kames's religious orthodoxy.

VI *Problem of Liberty and Necessity*

The first part of *Essays* concludes with the most notorious piece of the collection. Entitled "Of Liberty and Necessity," this essay almost cost Kames his position on the Scottish bench and gave ammunition to those who would link him with the Great Infidel, David Hume. Criticism was so severe and Kames's position was so insecure that he substantially modified the essay in a later edition. Oddly enough, those who linked Kames with Hume because of this essay could not have picked a more unlikely comparison; for Kames's argument depends on an observable and inevitable chain of cause and effect between objects.

Briefly, Kames argues for necessity in human actions. God permits man to think he is free and therefore a morally responsible agent, but man really has no control over his behavior. At first glance, Kames's theory seems naïve; but it must be considered in relation to a paradox which has long bewildered theologians—the order of providence and human responsibility. Kames, who once again attempts the role of compromiser, prefers paradox to the distortion of truth. Neither the extreme of necessitarianism nor that of absolute liberty explains the actual experience of man.

For the deistically inclined Kames, order in the universe demanded final causality. And, although the authority of the final-cause argument had been questioned by writers from Bacon to Hume, Kames preferred to maintain belief in such an order, pleasing in every way and presided over by a beneficent Deity: "Clearly he wished to remain in the camp of the cosmic optimists despite all the logic marshalled against the position he adopted."[10] Final cause, in Kames's view, operates according to an absolute necessity and therefore precludes free will. In the physical order, such movement toward a predetermined end is revealed in the cycle of life. Kames maintains that similar necessity exists in the moral order, a necessity seen most clearly in the relationship between motive and action:

Comparing together the moral and the natural world, every thing is as much the result of established laws in the one as in the other. There is nothing in the whole universe that can properly be called contingent, that may be or may not be; nothing loose and fluctuating in any part of nature; but every motion in the natural, and every determination and action in the moral world, are directed by immutable laws: so that, whilst these laws remain in their force, not the smallest link of the universal chain of causes and effects can be broken, nor any one thing be otherways than it is. (181–82)

No man can be conceived to act without some principle leading him to action. All our principles of action resolve into *desires* and *aversions;* for nothing can prompt us to move or exert ourselves in any shape, but what presents some object to be either pursued or avoided. A motive is an object so operating upon the mind, as to produce either desire or aversion. Now, liberty as opposed to moral necessity, must signify a power in the mind, of acting without or against motives; that is to say, a power of acting without any view, purpose or design, and even of acting in contradiction to our own desires and aversions, or to all our principles of action; which power, besides that no man was ever conscious of it, seems to be an absurdity altogether inconsistent with a rational nature. (174–75)

Like the Deists, Kames ignores the problem of evil, preferring to explain all activity which man is not always able to understand as the operation of Providence.

Man's conviction about his freedom to act, therefore, is a delusion, a deception permitted by God. Kames justifies such deceptiveness on the part of a supposedly beneficent deity by again making an analogy between the moral and the physical orders. The slightest reflection, he declares, reveals that man's external senses may be deceived. As Locke had demonstrated, many qualities apparently inherent in an object are actually subjective. Deception in the moral order should be, therefore, no more difficult to accept than that in the physical order.

VII   *The Nature of Belief*

In part III of *Essays* Kames examines seven problems currently being debated: "Of Belief," "Of the Idea of Self and of Personal Identity," "Of the Authority of Our Senses," "Of Our Idea of Power," "Of Our Knowledge of Future Events," "Of Our

Dread of Supernatural Powers in the Dark," and "Of Our Knowledge of the Deity." He approaches all of these problems from a common-sense point of view, and his solutions therefore depend a great deal upon the theory of man's affective consciousness which he has worked out in Part I. Four of the essays treat subjects then being hotly debated after the questionings of Locke, Berkeley, and Hume. In the final essay, Kames assembles all of his common-sense arguments in a defense of natural theology.

In "Of Belief" Kames turns his attention once again to the philosophy of David Hume. Like him, Kames considers belief a feeling rather than an intellectual assent; but he is unwilling to make belief simply a certain kind of sense impression. In the *Treatise of Human Nature,* Hume had equated belief with a lively or vivid impression:

> Thus it appears, that the *belief* or *assent,* which always attends the memory and senses, is nothing but the vivacity of those perceptions they present; and that this alone distinguishes them from the imagination. To believe is in this case to feel an immediate impression of the senses, or a repetition of that impression in the memory. 'Tis merely the force and liveliness of the perception, which constitutes the first act of the judgment.[11]

> An opinion, therefore, or belief may be most accurately defin'd, A LIVELY IDEA RELATED TO OR ASSOCIATED WITH A PRESENT IMPRESSION.[12]

Kames takes issue with Hume; and, while he never explicitly defines belief, Kames seems to consider it a separate action of the mind, an affective response not necessarily produced by a lively impression: "I have a high opinion of this author's acuteness and penetration; but no authority can prevail with me to embrace such a doctrine. . . . There is a certain peculiar manner of perceiving objects and conceiving propositions, which, being a simple feeling, cannot be described, but is expressed by the word belief" (222, 227).

For Kames, belief and a lively impression are two modifications of perception which may or may not occur concurrently. He agrees with Hume that belief, once achieved, will be accompanied by a lively impression; but he does not agree that all lively impressions produce belief. Kames can argue, for example, that poetry and drama may give a more lively impression than history; but they may not therefore produce belief (222). In *Elements of Criticism* Kames addresses himself once more to the problem of belief from the point of view of esthetics to determine how art may produce the illusion of life. Faced with the fact that poetry and drama often *do* produce belief, he works out a theory of "ideal presence" which makes belief in art the product of its accurate imitation of real life.

VIII *The Unifying Principles of Human Nature*

In the next three essays of Part II Kames attempts to defend the existence of three traditional principles which skepticism had challenged: personal identity, substance, and causation. His arguments in all three cases can be reduced to common-sense positions. In Essay II, "Of the Idea of Self and Personal Identity," Kames opposes Hume's theory that man's knowledge is limited to the impressions he receives from the five senses. Hume maintains that this limitation of knowledge precludes the philosophical demonstration of a self which continues to exist essentially unchanged. Kames's answer to Hume is simply an affirmation, based, as we have come to expect, on feeling:

It is an undoubted truth, that [man] has an original feeling, or consciousness of himself, and of his existence; which, for the most part, accompanies every one of his impressions and ideas, and every action of his mind and body. . . . It is this perception, or consciousness of self, carried through all the different stages of life, and all the variety of action, which is the foundation of *personal identity*. It is, by means of this perception, that I consider myself to be the same person, in all varieties of fortune, and every change of circumstance.

The main purpose of this short essay, is to introduce an observation, that it is not by any argument or reasoning, I conclude myself to be the same person, I was ten years ago. This conclusion rests entirely upon the feeling of identity, which accompanies me through all my changes, and which is the only connecting principle, that binds together, all the various thoughts and actions of my life. (231-34)

Kames's first concern in Essay III, "Of the Authority of Our Senses," is to clarify the apparent contradiction between his argument in the essay on liberty, that the senses may be deceived, and the subject of this essay. He explains that, in the earlier essay, he had been talking about exceptions to the authority of the senses that were caused by such factors as distance or illness, and that in general the senses are reliable guides to truth. Kames thus adds another common-sense proposition to his theory of knowledge: "... when we have nothing but our senses to direct our conduct, with regard to external objects, it would be strange, if there should be any just ground, for a general distrust of them" (239).

Philosophically speaking, substance is the counterpart in the objective order of self in the subjective order, and it accounts for the unity of the object. As was mentioned at the beginning of this chapter, the more or less uncritical acceptance of substance, which had characterized traditional philosophy, suffered sharp blows from Locke, Berkeley, and Hume. While not denying the existence of substance, Locke questioned whether man could have any knowledge of it. Berkeley, impressed by Locke's distinction between primary and secondary qualities of objects —qualities which are really part of the object (primary) and those which are transferred from subject to object (secondary) —carried Locke's logic a step further by maintaining that all qualities are subjective and hence that man cannot know anything other than his own ideas. Hume completed the logical process by questioning whether ideas are anything more than somewhat faded impressions.

Kames first attempts to resolve the whole problem by denying that it exists. His argument offers a marvelous illustration of the logical fallacy of begging the question. He assumes that quality and substance can be defined into existence:

'Tis not a little surprising, that philosophers, who discourse so currently of *qualities*, should affect so much doubt and hesitation about *substance;* seeing these are relative ideas, and imply each other. For what other reason do we call figure a quality, but that we perceive it, not as a separate existence, but as belonging to something that is figured; and which thing we call *substance*, because it is not a property of any other thing, but is a thing which subsists by itself, or has an independent existence. (247)

He then scores Locke for being so timid about substance, once again assuming that the definition of something makes it a reality: "He [Locke] observes that we have no clear nor distinct idea of substance. If he means, that we have no clear nor distinct idea of substance abstracted from its properties, the thing is so true, that we can form no idea of substance at all, abstracted from its properties. But it is also true, that we can form no idea of properties, abstracted from a substance" (251).

Berkeley errs, according to Kames, because his ideas violate common sense: "The doctor's fundamental proposition is, that we can perceive nothing but our own ideas or perceptions ... tho', in so bold an undertaking, as that of annihilating the whole universe, his own mind excepted, he had no reason to hope, that an assertion, so singular, and so contradictory to common sense and feeling, would be taken upon his word" (257–58). And Hume is criticized for oversimplifying human experience by failing to distinguish those impressions which are conscious and become ideas from those which are not conscious. Kames holds fast to this mentalistic psychology despite the fact that it conflicts with his own ideas about internal senses.

Essay IV, "Of Our Idea of Power," which deals with the problem of causation, presents the most striking contrast between rationalism and common sense to be found in *Essays*. As we have seen in the section on liberty and necessity, Kames is a determinist. In the present essay he unequivocally founds his determinism upon a common-sense proposition; every cause has within it the power to produce certain predictable effects. Kames begins by rejecting the arguments of Locke and Clarke, who tried to explain causation rationally. Both, Kames declares, have begged the question by assuming that everything which exists must have been caused to exist. Kames replies with a statement that could have been written by Hume: " ... there does not appear to me any contradiction in the ... proposition, that a thing may begin to exist without a cause" (275).

If reason cannot explain causality, how does it happen that all men have strong convictions about cause and effect? Hume, Kames points out, states that the answer lies in the human imagination and in the effect of custom and habit upon it:

The author of the treatise of human nature, has employed a world of reasoning, in searching for the foundation of our idea of power and of necessary connection. And, after all his anxious researches, he can make no more of it, but "That the idea of necessary connection, alias *power* or *energy,* arises from a number of instances, of one thing always following another, which connects them in the imagination; whereby we can readily foretel [*sic*] the existence of the one from the appearance of the other." And he pronounces, "That this connection can never be suggested from any one of these instances, surveyed in all possible lights and positions." Thus he places the essence of necessary connection, or power, upon that propensity, which custom produces, to pass from an object to the idea of its usual attendant. And from these premises, he draws a conclusion of a very extraordinary nature, and which he himself acknowledges to be not a little paradoxical. His words are: "Upon the whole, necessity is something that exists in the mind, not in objects; nor is it possible for us even to form the most distant idea of it, considered as a quality in bodies. The efficacy or energy in causes, is neither placed in the causes themselves, nor in the Deity, nor in the concurrence of these two principles; but belongs entirely to the soul, which considers the union of two or more objects in all past instances. 'Tis here that the real power of causes is placed, along with their connection and necessity." (282–84)

This solution, of course, is not acceptable to Kames, who is convinced that cause and effect really exist in the objective order. Common sense provides the answer. What assures man that every effect must have a cause and conversely that every cause has the power to produce certain effects is not reason, but sense and feeling. "Fond of arguments drawn from the nature of things, we are too apt to apply such arguments without discretion; and to call that demonstration, which, at bottom, is nothing but a conviction from sense and feeling. Our perceptions, which work silently, and without effort, are apt to be overlooked; and we vainly imagine, we can demonstrate every proposition, which we perceive to be true" (276).

IX   *God and Evil*

"Of Our Knowledge of the Deity," the final chapter of *Essays,* brings together several of Kames's principles—antirationalism, common sense, and cosmic optimism—in an attempt to persuade

the reader of a truth which Kames considers centrally important for human experience. In good eighteenth-century fashion,
he objects to the metaphysical proofs for the existence of God
on grounds as egalitarian as they are antirationalistic. Why,
Kames asks, should one demand that people base their faith on
a series of rational arguments which the vast majority of them
cannot understand? "Is the knowledge of God, then, reserved
for persons of great study and deep thinking? Is a vail thrown
over the eyes of the rest of mankind?" (315). On the contrary,
the common man need only become aware of his own feelings
to be convinced of the existence of God: "To substitute feeling
in place of reason and demonstration, may seem to put the evidence of the Deity upon too low a footing. But human reason
is not so mighty an affair, as philosophers vainly pretend. It
affords very little aid, in making original discoveries. The comparing of things together, and directing our inferences from
feeling and experience, are its proper province" (339–40).

If man must attempt to reason to the existence of God, he
must also realize that none of these arguments convinces of itself; it merely moves the feeling to assent: "... it is an error,
common to the bulk of writers, to substitute reason for feeling.
The faculty of perception, working silently, and without effort,
is generally overlookt. And we must find a reason for every
thing we judge to be true; tho' the truth of the proposition
often depends, not upon reasoning, but upon mere feeling"
(349). The best argument, Kames adds, is the argument from
causality. Man does not have the power to cause himself or the
natural world; therefore a first cause, or God, must exist. Kames
takes on David Hume for the last time in *Essays* to object to his
handling of the First Cause argument in the "Natural History of
Religion." To Hume's declaration that one can only attribute to
cause what the effect contains, and, since the world is imperfect,
so must its cause be imperfect, Kames replies, "... happily for man,
where reason fails him, perception and feeling come to his assistance" (357).

The Deist argument for order in the universe is often criticized for ignoring the problem of evil in both the physical and
the moral order. Kames concludes his essay on the existence of
God by considering evil, which seemingly places limitations on

the deity. His suggestions sound a good deal like those of Pope in *An Essay on Man*. First of all, Kames says, if we look closely enough at any problem, we will discover that all is for the best in the world. What we think is evil actually turns out to be good: "Our discoveries ascertain us more and more of the benevolence of the Deity, by unfolding beautiful final causes without number; while the appearances of evil intention gradually vanish, like a mist, after the sun breaks out" (362–63). The great chain of being provides an answer to the problem of physical evil. The world is filled with a variety of creatures ranging "from the most grovelling, to the most glorious." (365). Imperfection in certain of these creatures confirms rather than disproves an ultimate order. In the moral order, evil is simply a delusion. God disposes all actions according to his Providence, and man should not question his ways.

The Deist prayer which concludes *Essays* was composed by Kames's friend, Hugh Blair. In sentiments which seem naïve today, but which apparently offered great consolation to eighteenth-century readers, Blair lyrically summarizes Kames's natural and moral philosophy:

For do not all these wonders, *O Eternal Mind!* Sovereign Architect of all! form a hymn to thy praise? If in the dead inanimate works of nature, thou art seen; if in the verdure of the fields, and the azure of the skies, the ignorant rustic admires thy creative power; how blind must that man be, who, looking into his own nature, contemplating this living structure, this moral frame, discerns not thy forming hand? What various and complicated machinery is here! and regulated with what exquisite art! Whilst man pursues happiness as his chief aim, thou bendest self-love into the social direction. Thou infusest the generous principle, which makes him feel for sorrows not his own.... Thy divine hand, thus strongly, drew the connecting tye, and linked man to man, by a sympathetic power; that nothing might be solitary or desolate in thy world; but all tend and work toward mutual association. . . . . All things are by thee preordained, great Mover of all! Throughout the wide expanse, every living creature runs a destined course.... (Man) imagines himself free, yet is under the bonds of necessity. He discovers himself to be a necessary agent, and yet continues to act as he were free.... Neither imperfection nor malice dwell with thee. Thou appointest as salutary, what we lament as painful. What mortals term sin, thou pronouncest to be only error. For moral evil vanishes, in some measure, from before thy more perfect sight: and as, at the beginning of days, thou saw'st, so thou see'st, and pronouncest still, that *every thing thou has made is good.* (389–94)

Essays on the Principles of Morality and Natural Religion can be described as the systematic exposition of a moral philosophy which Kames later combines with empirical psychology in working out his theory of criticism in *Elements of Criticism,* as will be seen in the following chapter. It is the statement of a stalwart believer who confronted a new philosophy which questioned his very reason for existence. As Ian Ross has so astutely commented, in speaking of Lord Kames's mind: "It was a mind capable of no great philosophical acumen or much sophistication of statement, but rather of an iron grasp of a few ideas and a tenacious maintenance of the position to which they led. The significant point, however, is that Henry Home was aware of the moral and metaphysical writings of his contemporaries, and that iron-clad mind of his went churning on into the new seas of thought revealed by Berkeley and Hume."[13]

At the beginning of this chapter, we noted certain key philosophical developments which led to *Essays.* Kames's book can also be considered part of a larger pattern in eighteenth-century thought which James McCosh has called "The Scottish Philosophy." McCosh describes the three major characteristics of the school and its value in the history of thought, and his ideas provide a useful outline of Kames's method, as well as suggesting some of the topics to which Kames addresses himself in *Elements of Criticism.* The "Scottish Philosophy" characteristically:

proceeds on the method of observation, professedly and really; ... employs self-consciousness as the method of investigation; ... by the observation of consciousness [reaches] principles ... which are prior to and independent of experience. ... But the great merit of the Scottish philosophy lies in the large body of truth which it has—if not discovered—at least settled on a foundation which can never be moved. It has added very considerably to our knowledge of the human mind, bringing out to view the characteristics of mental as distinguished from material action; throwing light on perception through the senses; offering valuable observations on the intellec--

tual powers, and on the association of ideas; furnishing, if not ultimate, yet very useful provisional classifications of the mental faculties; unfolding many of the peculiarities of man's moral and emotional nature, of his conscience, and of his taste for the beautiful; resolving many complex mental phenomena into their elements; throwing aside by its independent research a host of traditional errors which had been accumulating for ages; and, above all, establishing certain primary truths as a foundation on which to rear other truths, and as a backwater to resist the assaults of scepticism.[14]

CHAPTER 3

Elements of Criticism: Psychology and Art

IN the introduction to his recent edition of William Blake's poetry, Professor Vivian de Sola Pinto observes that the ideals and values of the later eighteenth century in England can be summarized in the title of a book published in 1787 by one Dr. John Trussler, *The Way to be Rich and Respectable.* "It was," says Pinto, "the England of George III and George IV, a nation dominated by what Matthew Arnold called 'impregnable philistinism.' Its prophets were Bacon, Newton, and Locke, and it lived in a solid, material universe of Hard Facts, the universe of Mr. Gradgrind. It was the age of purple-faced squires, pluralistic clergymen, hanging judges, press gangs, and debtors' prisons...."[1] While Professor Pinto's generalization hits disconcertingly near the bone, it does not take into account the constant attempts in this period to remedy these cultural ills, to cultivate in purple-faced squires that enigmatic thing called "taste". In Scotland, Adam Smith and Hugh Blair lectured at Glasgow and Edinburgh on rhetoric and *belles-lettres.* Thomas Sheridan was imported to educate native-speaking Scots on the proprieties and elegancies of the British tongue—southern variety. Countless essays appeared on the nature of taste and on methods of acquiring it. If nothing else, *Elements of Criticism,* Lord Kames's most widely read and influential book, composed for the single purpose of improving taste, offered to Mr. Gradgrind suggestions for making his philistinism about art and literature at least a bit more refined.

Elements of Criticism—Kames deliberately omitted the presumptuous definite article from the title—appeared in 1762, and it soon became a popular handbook on criticism and rhetoric. Hume doubted that it would sell and Voltaire publicly maligned it, but within Kames's lifetime the book went through five editions, each with "corrections and additions," and ultimately had a total of eleven English editions. The book was even more popular in America, where it went through thirty-one printings.[2] A German translation was made in 1763, and Kames's ideas influenced the esthetic theories of such German critics as Lessing, Herder, and Schiller.[3] A notice of *Elements* for April, 1762, gives us some idea of how well the book was received: "[Kames's] accurate criticism . . . if we mistake not, will render him in the critical art, what Bacon, Locke, and Newton, are in philosophy—the parent of regulated taste, the creator of metaphysical criticism, the first interpreter of our feelings and of the voice of nature, and the lawgiver of capricious genius, upon principles too evident to be controverted."[4]

The popularity of the book belies its difficulty:

If Kame's book called for interpretation and elucidation in its own time, it requires even more explanation now. Not only did he force the reader, by a very forbidding scheme of presentation, to carry with him to the end of the argument the principles and proofs laid down at the beginning; he also expected a knowledge of contemporary philosophy, and he did not see fit to outline for his reader every one of the many literary and philosophical controversies of that day to which he made covert allusion. Furthermore, although he himself was a rhetorician and was considered by at least one of his successors to be a model of the "concise style," his manner of expression was peculiarly his own. Nor is the reader's path made smoother by his excursions into all fields related to literature in his exhaustive search for principles of composition and art.[5]

At first glance, the book seems a potpourri of fashionable eighteenth-century critical topics—taste, beauty, sublimity, wit, narration, and description. Along with elements of criticism, it contains elements of philosophy, rhetoric, and esthetics. But a closer examination reveals several distinct patterns of organization, as Helen Randall has pointed out. She divides *Elements* into six parts: (1) Fundamental principles of human nature (chapters I-II); (2) Principles of the arts (chapters III-XV); (3) Transitional chapters on minor principles (chapters XVI–XVII); (4) Rhetoric and poetic (chapters XVIII–XXIII); (5) Gardening and architecture (chapter XXIV); and (6)

Standard of taste (chapter XXV).[6] The next two chapters of this present study more or less follow Miss Randall's divisions. This chapter, "Psychology and Art," considers the close relation which Kames observes between philosophy and esthetics. The following chapter, "The Nature of Style," considers the subtantial modification of traditional rhetorical theory which Kames felt the new philosophy demanded.

I *The Meaning of Nature*

Perhaps the most important organizing principle in *Elements of Criticism,* one which informs all of Kames's theories about rhetoric and esthetics, is the principle of "naturalism." Readers familiar with eighteenth-century intellectual history will recognize in it one of the era's most widely accepted bases for taste: nature as esthetic norm. Nature, like so many other critical terms such as "judgment," "romanticism," and "wit," has no single meaning in the period.[7] For critical traditionalists early in the century, to follow nature often meant the almost slavish imitation of a Classical model in such genres as epic and tragedy. For Kames and other critics later in the period, however, longevity did not automatically guarantee that a particular work contained nature. To merit recognition, a work had to reflect accurately human nature and experience. Art, therefore, becomes at its best a faithful mirror of reality. Throughout *Elements,* Kames employs this principle of naturalism to establish the rules for esthetics and for rhetoric, and to judge a particular literary performance.

In the introduction to the book, Kames gives a succinct exposition of his theory of artistic naturalism in objecting to the unscientific critical theory of Bossu, a celebrated seventeenth-century French critic: "Bossu . . . gives many rules; but can discover no better foundation for any of them, than the practice merely of Homer and Virgil, supported by the authority of Aristotle: strange, that in so long a work, the concordance or discordance of these rules with human nature, should never once have entered his thoughts."[8] Critical theory, whose principles will encourage the fine arts to become a force for order in society, must proceed on a more scientific basis than does Bossu. Its principles must derive from a knowledge of human psychology—"by studying the sensitive part of human nature, and [by] learning what objects are naturally agreeable, and what are naturally disagreeable" (I, 7-8). The development of the esthetic sense, or taste, thus parallels the development of the moral sense we have noted in the preceding chapter. Education encourages man's instinctive response to natural objects to become a learned response to artificial objects: "Thus the fine arts, like morals, become a rational science; and, like morals, may be cultivated to a high degree of refinement" (I, 8).

In addition to establishing his methodology for what might be called "rational criticism," Lord Kames also says some interesting things about esthetic pleasure in his introduction to *Elements of Criticism.* Following the lead of Addison, he locates such pleasures midway between the purely intellectual and the purely physical; and he limits them to the sense experience of the eye and ear: "Their mixt nature and middle place betwixt organic and intellectual pleasures, qualify them to associate with both: beauty heightens all the organic feelings, as well as those that are intellectual" (I, 3). Valuable for their own sake, such esthetic pleasures can also have a quasi-cathartic function, balancing organic or intellectual excesses. Most importantly, however, a taste for the pleasures of the ear and eye leads to a taste for purely mental pleasures, a process which reveals once again the operation of a providential design moving the mind "by gentle steps from the most grovelling corporeal pleasures, for which only it is fitted in the beginning of life, to those refined and sublime pleasures which are suited to its maturity" (I, 5). Kames suggests here the associational chain essential to his critical theory.

II *Association and Art*

The first two chapters of *Elements,* "Perceptions and Ideas in a Train" and "Emotions and Passions," contain most of Kames's ideas about human psychology and form the theoretical basis for his subsequent discussion of such esthetic problems as beauty and sublimity. In Chapter I, Kames describes the most fundamental principle of his theory of the mind, the principle of association, which in his view explains the relation of ideas and feelings. In Chapter II, he elaborates upon the nature of human feeling and suggests another important psychological principle—that of sympathy. It is largely in terms of these two principles, association and sympathy, that man experiences the beautiful. And through the perfect combination of these, an artist can produce in his audience that most esthetically satisfying state which Kames calls "ideal presence."

Adopted from the philosophical system of David Hume, the principle of association underlies man's experience of himself and the outside world through sense impressions, and his subsequent reflection upon such experience. Like Hume, Kames reasons that all human knowledge originates in the senses. Unlike Hume, however, as we have seen in the preceding chapter, Kames maintains that man possesses both internal and external senses. The external senses provide knowledge of physical reality; the internal, knowledge of such abstract realities as morality and beauty. Discrete sense experiences are ordered and structured according to the principle of association:

A man while awake is sensible of a continued train of perceptions and ideas passing in his mind. It requires no activity on his part to carry on the train: nor can he at will add to the train any idea that has no connection with it. At the same time we learn from daily experience, that a train of thought is not merely casual: and if it depend not upon will, nor upon chance, by what law is it governed? The question is of importance in the science of human nature; and I promise beforehand, that it will be found of great importance in the fine arts.

It appears that the relations by which things are linked together, have a great influence in directing the train of thought; because we find by experience, that ideas are connected in the mind precisely as their objects are externally. Taking a view of external objects, we see that they are not more remarkable by their inherent properties than by their various relations; for we cannot any where extend our view without perceiving things connected together by certain relations: one thing perceived to be a cause, is connected with its several effects; some things are connected by contiguity in time, others by contiguity in place; some are connected by resemblance, some by contrast; some go before, some follow: not a single thing appears solitary and altogether devoid of connection; the only difference is, that some are intimately connected, some more slightly; some near, some at a distance. (I, 21–23)

Man's notion of reality outside himself, his notion of what is natural, depends on this series of relations.

Several implications for the fine arts follow from the association of ideas. First of all, there is a direct relationship between a pattern of ideas and pleasure. Order, conceived associationally, offers the key to both natural and esthetic pleasure. The mind is pleased with those impressions and ideas which are liveliest or most immediate, and by those which are most intimately and easily associated. "It appears then that we are framed by nature to relish order and connection. When an object is introduced by a proper connection, we are conscious of a certain pleasure arising from that circumstance . . . the mind proceeds with alacrity down a flowing river, and with the same alacrity from a whole to its parts, or from a principle to its accessories; but in the contrary direction, it is sensible of a sort of retrograde motion, which is unpleasant (I, 32–33). Because of this natural association, man derives most pleasure when he first contemplates a whole and then its parts. The attempt to pass from part to whole invariably produces "a sense of disorder" (I, 29).

To produce a pleasure similar to that experienced in the natural order, the artist must recognize the principle of association and so construct his artificial works that they imitate its natural operation.[9] What Kames has in mind would be called "organic unity" by later literary critics.[10] Kames even uses the organic metaphor:

Every work of art that is conformable to the natural course of our ideas, is so far agreeable; and every work of art that reverses that course, is so far disagreeable. Hence it is required in every such work, that, like an organic system, it have its parts orderly arranged and mutually connected, bearing each of them a relation to the whole, some more intimate, some less, according to their definition: when due regard is paid to these particulars, we have a sense of just composition, and so far are pleased with the performance. (I, 35)

The unnatural in a work of art is that which violates the decorum of natural association. Kames criticizes Homer, Pindar, Horace, and Virgil for their "want of connection" (I, 36).

III *Sympathy as Esthetic Norm*

In Chapter II, Kames considers man's affective life, his emotions and passions as they relate once again to the natural and esthetic orders. The simple pleasure and pain connected with original impressions does not adequately explain human experience. Introspection reveals a more conscious level of feeling which we call "emotion" and "passion". Kames works out a distinction between these, one which turns on the more object-directed nature of passion; but he himself does not use the terms consistently in *Elements*. For purposes of understanding the critical theory, the distinction between simple pleasures and emotions suffices.

In sections III and IV of Chapter II, Kames points out two characteristics of human psychology which are extremely important for his critical theory: the principle of sympathy and the association of emotions.[11] Sympathy for Kames means something far more than pity; it is a principle which accounts for human communication.[12] According to the empirical tenets of the new philosophy, no such communication was possible. A gap which no amount of metaphysical speculation could successfully bridge existed between individual consciousness and the outside world. Man, trapped in the world of his own subjective experience, could know his own impressions, ideas and feelings, but never those of other men. Again, following the lead of David Hume, who treated the matter extensively in Book II of the *Treatise of Human Nature,* Kames proposes a theory of sympathy to explain how man bridges this philosophical gap.

Sympathy is not an intuitive process whereby we are constantly aware of another person's emotions. Its operation depends on that quality of liveliness in the object which Kames identifies with our most intense sensory experience. As we shall see below, Kames, operating in a mechanist tradition,[13] believes that in the natural order all emotions have their physical equivalent in such external signs as tone of voice, gesture, and facial expression. When these external signs produce in us a lively impression, they give us the key to another's emotional state; and we can then experience sympathy.

Kames's illustrations of the principle of sympathy are naïve but can also be instructive. In Part VI of Chapter II, entitled

"Of the Resemblance Emotions Bear to their Causes," where he attempts to pinpoint the precise emotional effect of certain external conditions, Kames is not at his best. What follows is almost Swiftian reductionism:

Motion in its different circumstances, is productive of feelings that resemble it: sluggish motion, for example, causeth a languid unpleasant feeling; slow uniform motion, a feeling calm and pleasant; and brisk motion, a lively feeling that rouses the spirits and promotes activity. A fall of water through rocks, raises in the mind a tumultuous confused agitation, extremely similar to its cause. When force is exerted with any effort, the spectator feels a similar effort as of force exerted within his mind. A large object swells the heart. An elevated object makes the spectator stand erect. (I, 227–28)

He declares that low sounds "bring down the mind" and that constraining clothing on others, and architecture not firmly footed can produce uneasiness in an observer.

In addition to this amusing mechanical equivalence of emotion and object, Kames does have some perceptive things to say about how the sympathetic principle enables us to participate in the experience of others. A display of courage, for example, stirs courageous feelings in a spectator; and any virtuous action can make us more inclined to virtue:

When we contemplate a virtuous action, which never fails to delight us and to prompt our love for the author, the mind is warmed and put into a tone similar to what inspired the virtuous action; and the propensity we have to such actions is so much enlivened, as to become for a time an actual emotion. (I, 77)

For another example, let us figure some grand and heroic action, highly agreeable to the spectator. Beside a singular veneration for the author, the spectator feels in himself an unusual dignity of character, which disposeth him to great and noble actions. And herein principally consists the extreme delight every one hath in the histories of conquerors and heroes. (I, 76)

In addition to being influenced by the principle of sympathy, our emotions also follow a pattern of association, just as ideas do. The artist who would imitate human nature must be aware of such association. An object which gives pleasure to the observer prompts him to react pleasurably to things surrounding the principal object. Affection for a man soon becomes affection for all his qualities, even in cases where these are not particularly pleasant in themselves. Thus "the wry neck of Alexander was imitated by his courtiers as a real beauty" (I, 82). And Lady Percy comments on how her husband Hotspur's speech impediment has become an object of admiration:

> By his light
> Did all the chivalry of England move,
> To do brave acts. He was indeed the glass,
> Wherein the noble youth did dress themselves.
> He had no legs that practis'd not his gait:
> And speaking thick, which Nature made his blemish,
> Became the accents of the valiant:
> For those who could speak slow and tardily,
> Would turn their own perfection to abuse,
> To seem like him.
>
> *Second Part, Henry IV*, Act II, Sc. 6 (I, 82)

"Diana is chaste, and not only her temple, but the very isicle which hangs on it, must partake of that property" (I, 83). Conversely, a painful emotion communicates displeasure to all surrounding objects, as when King John declares: "Fellow begone, I cannot brook thy sight/This news hath made thee a most ugly man." *King John,* Act III, Sc. 1 (I, 84).

IV *Ideal Presence: The Persuasive Power of Art*

Having laid the foundations of his critical theory in association and sympathy, Kames turns in Section VI to an important application of these principles to esthetics. Any critical theory which sets up nature as an ideal must eventually face the question of what to do about art which, no matter how it is qualified, still remains artificial. Some have ignored the fact that art pleases and have excluded the "makers" from the Commonwealth, but Kames wants no part in this deception. "Our passions," he declares, "as all the world know, are moved by fiction as well as by truth" (I, 109). To explain this paradox, he proposes what he calls "ideal presence." If a work of art is natural enough or lively enough, the audience is convinced that it is real. Kames recognizes here what Coleridge a half century later was to call the "willing suspension of disbelief." To persuade his audience, or to evoke from it a pleasurable response, therefore, the artist must imitate as closely as he can the associational and affective realities of human experience.

Kames discusses ideal presence as it relates both to ideas and emotions. It is, first of all, an experience possible outside of art, a kind of memory recall which Kames places between "real presence" and "reflective remembrance":

In contradistinction to real presence, ideal presence may properly be termed *a waking dream;* because, like a dream, it vanisheth upon the first reflection of our present situation: real presence, on the contrary, vouched by eye-sight, commands our belief, not only during the direct perception, but in reflecting afterward upon the object. And with respect to the distinction betwixt ideal presence and reflective remembrance, I give the following illustration. Two internal acts, both of them exertions of memory, are clearly distinguishable: when I think of an event as past, without forming any image, it is barely reflecting or remembering that I was an eye-witness: but when I recall the event so distinctly as to form a complete image of it, I perceive it ideally as passing in my presence; and this ideal perception is an act of intuition, into which reflection enters not more than into an act of sight. (I, 113–14)

But ideal presence can also be produced by the vivid presentation in oratory, writing or painting of some experience we have never had: "A lively and accurate description of an important event, raises in me ideas, not less distinct than if I had been originally an eye-witness: I am insensibly transformed into a spectator; and have an impression as every incident were passing in my presence" (I, 115).

Again the quality of liveliness is stressed; for to please, art must successfully imitate the most intense kind of natural experience. And emotions as well as ideas can be raised by fiction in much the same manner: "The power of language to raise emotions, depends entirely on the raising such lively and distinct images as are here described: the reader's passions are never sensibly moved, till he be thrown into a kind of reverie; in which state, losing the consciousness of self, and of reading, his present occupation, he conceives every incident as passing in his presence, precisely as if he were an eye-witness" (I, 117).

The meeting of Hector and Andromache, and the death of King Lear can produce emotions in the reader or in the audience at least as intense as those the historian Tacitus creates when he describes the death of Otho.

V *Language and Action: The Relative Value of the Arts*

In the last part of Section VI, Kames attempts to determine the relative value of the arts, or, in Kames's terms, to determine how effectively the various arts produce the illusion of reality. Lessing, the great German critic, was to give this subject its most profound theoretical exposition in *Laokoön* (1766) when he discussed the mutually exclusive characteristics of poetry and painting. For Kames, of course, drama can best produce ideal presence because it can truly imitate reality through the combination of language and action. For this reason Kames takes most of his illustrations for various critical points from drama.

But our experience testifies that the illusion of reality can also be produced in an audience by language alone, independent of action, as in the reading of poetry and drama. Painting, on the other hand, can produce this illusion through action alone independent of language: "That words independent of action have the same power in a less degree, every one of sensibility must have felt: a good tragedy will extort tears in private, though not so forcibly as upon the stage. This power belongs also to painting: a good historical picture makes a deeper impression than can be made by words, though not equal to what is made by theatrical action" (I, 121-22).

Painting and language, however, do not produce the same intensity of passion or the same vividness of impression. In a provocative passage which anticipates Lessing, Kames declares that language can more perfectly imitate reality than painting because language can reproduce actual experience which takes place in time and is thus characterized by succession. To arouse the passions, particularly the sympathetic passions, a succession of impressions is required. Painting, which exists in space rather than in time, is characteristically static rather than successive:

It must not however be thought, that our passions can be raised by painting to such a height as can be done by words: of all the successive incidents that concur to produce a great event, a picture has the choice but of one, because it is confined to a single instant of time; and though the impression it makes is the deepest that can be made instantaneously, yet seldom can a passion be raised to any height in an instant, or by a single impression: it was observed above, that our passions, those especially of the sympathetic kind, require a succession of impressions; and for that reason, reading, and still more acting, have greatly the advantage, by the opportunity of reiterating impressions without end. (I, 122-23)

Some of the most interesting parts of *Elements of Criticism* deal with the practical application of critical principles. In connection with his discussion of ideal presence, Kames takes up the use of epic machinery which he feels has marred heroic poetry from Homer to Pope. The serious artist, Kames declares, must avoid what is unnatural if he wishes to move his audience. Although the improbable does produce an emotional effect, it is one of novelty rather than of sympathy:

I appeal to the discerning reader, whether this observation be not applicable to the machinery introduced by Tasso and by Voltaire: such machinery is not only in itself cold and uninteresting, but is remarkably hurtful, by giving an air of fiction to the whole composition. A burlesque poem, such as the Lutrin or the Dispensary, may employ machinery with success; for these poems, though they assume the air of history, give entertainment chiefly by their pleasant and ludicrous pictures, to which machinery contributes: it is not the aim of such a poem, to raise our sympathy in any considerable degree; and for that reason, a strict imitation of nature is not required. A poem professedly ludicrous, may employ machinery to great advantage; and the more extravagant the better. (I, 130-31)

Voltaire did not take kindly to Kames's criticism of his epic, as his review of *Elements of Criticism* demonstrated.

VI   *The Association of Emotions and Decorum*

In Part IV of Chapter II, "Coexistent emotions and passions," Kames, who again reveals his view that nature is essentially mechanical, declares that the experience of an object or action in the natural order produces an attendant emotion. Rather than being an esemplastic structure, as Coleridge would describe it in *Biographia Literaria,* the human mind contains discrete impressions and discrete emotions. Like impressions, emotions are related to one another through resemblance, contiguity, or causality. A judgment about the harmony or discord of a particular experience is also a judgment about emotional association:

> Two pleasant emotions that are similar, readily unite when they are coexistent; and the pleasure felt in the union, is the sum of the two pleasures: the same emotions in succession, are far from making the same figure; because the mind at no instant of the succession is conscious of more than a single emotion. This doctrine may aptly be illustrated by a landscape comprehending hills, vallies, plains, rivers, trees, *etc.:* the emotions produced by these several objects, being similar in a high degree, as falling in easily and sweetly with the same tone of mind, are in conjunction extremely pleasant. This multiplied effect is felt from objects even of different senses; as where a landscape is conjoined with the music of birds and odor of flowers; and depends partly on the resemblance of the emotions and partly on the connection of their causes: whence it follows, that the effect must be the greatest, where the causes are intimately connected and the emotions perfectly similar. (I, 161–62)

Again, emotional association is most interesting insofar as it applies to art. Milton, for example, weakens the effect of his forlorn waste in *Paradise Lost* by using beautiful images to describe it:

> Seest thou yon dreary plain, forlorn and wild,
> The seat of desolation, void of light,
> Save what the glimmering of these livid flames
> Casts pale and dreadful? (I, 167)

Kames is proposing the old critical commonplace of decorum which insists that style and content must complement one another, but he is expressing it in psychological terms: "... ascending smoke in a calm morning is improper in a picture full of violent action: the emotion of stillness and tranquillity inspired by the former, accords not with the lively and animated emotion inspired by the latter. A parterre, partly ornamented, partly in disorder, produces a mixt feeling of the same sort. Two great armies in act to engage, mix the dissimilar emotions of grandeur and terror" (I, 167).

Vocal music is an artistic form which Kames maintains should follow the principle of the association of emotions. He has the rather curious notion that music produces only pleasant emotions!—an obviously pre-Bartokian, pre-Wagnerian point of view. Thus, since language and music produce distinct emotional responses, their successful combination obviously requires a harmony of emotion which only pleasing language can produce:

...in vocal music, the intimate connection of sense and sound rejects dissimilar emotions, those especially that are opposite: similar emotions produced by the sense and the sound go naturally into union; and at the same time are concordant or harmonious; but dissimilar emotions, forced into union by these causes intimately connected, obscure each other, and are also unpleasant by discordance.

These premises make it easy to determine what sort of poetical compositions are fitted for music. It is evident that no poem expressing the sentiments of any disagreeable passion is proper. (I, 175)

Kames introduces for special censure that prime example of impropriety, French and Italian opera, an artistic form which pays not the least regard to decorum. He does not consider opera as serious vocal music, however, since its pleasure derives almost entirely from the music, "scarce at all from the sentiments" (I, 178).

VII   *Modes of Esthetic Perception: Beauty*

In chapters III, IV, and VI of *Elements of Criticism,* Lord Kames turns his attention to three related topics in eighteenth-century literary criticism—beauty, grandeur/sublimity, and novelty. Addison, who adopted the categories from Locke, had discussed them at length in *The Spectator* No. 412 as part of the pleasures of the imagination under the headings of the "great," the "uncommon," and the "beautiful." Hume and Hutcheson—indeed, all the critics who operated within the new empirical and psychological framework—organized their discussions of esthetic response using categories similar to these. For all of them, including Kames, the esthetic response was more emotional than intellectual. The beautiful, the sublime, and the novel, in other words, were degrees of feeling rather than qualities in external objects. Appreciation of beauty, like that of truth and goodness, depended on the development of a refined sensibility. Kames could appreciate the old scholastic triad of the beautiful, the good, and the true; but he does so in an emotional and intuitive context which strict rationalism would have found highly objectionable.

The subject of beauty arises at several points in *Elements of Criticism* before Chapter III. In the second part of Chapter II, "Emotions and passions as pleasant and painful, agreeable and disagreeable," Kames makes a distinction which informs his extensive discussion of the subject in Chapter III. Beauty, he declares, is both objective and subjective—objective, in relating to certain formal qualities in external objects; subjective, in relating to a certain kind of emotional response: "Viewing a fine garden, I perceive it to be beautiful or agreeable; and I consider the beauty or agreeableness as belonging to the object, or as one of its qualities. Again, when I turn my attention from the garden to what passes in my mind, I am conscious of a pleasant emotion of which the garden is the cause. The pleasure here is felt, as a quality, not of the garden, but of the emotion produced by it" (I, 134). He makes essentially the same point in Chapter III: "Beauty therefore, which for its existence depends upon the percipient as much as upon the object perceived, cannot be an inherent property in either: what else then can it be, but a perception in the mind occasioned by certain objects? And hence it is wittily observed by the poet, that beauty is not in the countenance, but in the lover's eye" (I, 271–72).

Esthetics faced a serious challenge in the mid-eighteenth century from Utilitarianism, a philosophy which would consider beautiful only what was useful. Numbered among its most prominent exponents were David Hume and Adam Smith. Kames agreed with the Utilitarians that pleasure could be found in the contemplation of an object achieving its end. Man could call the beauty of means fitted to end "relative beauty,"—beauty intelligible only in relation to other objects or actions. An appreciation of purposefulness can make beautiful what is intrinsically ugly: "... an old Gothic tower that has no beauty in itself, appears beautiful, considered as proper to defend against an enemy: a dwelling-house void of all regularity, is however beautiful in the view of convenience; and the want of form or symmetry in a tree, will not prevent its appearing beautiful, if it be known to produce good fruit" (I, 256).

[72]

But experience is not limited to relative beauty, according to Kames. Man can also speak of "intrinsic beauty," a response not related to consideration of final cause. While relative beauty is an experience growing out of reflection, intrinsic beauty needs only the operation of the senses: ". . . to perceive the beauty of a spreading oak or of a flowing river, no more is required but singly an act of vision" (I, 254-55). Kames then distinguishes a more intense degree of beauty which combines both the intrinsic and the relative: "When these two beauties concur in any object, it appears delightful: every member of the human body possesses both in a high degree: the slender make of a horse destined for running, pleases every taste; partly from symmetry, and partly from utility" (I, 256).

Intrinsic beauty in the natural order is characterized by regularity and simplicity, uniformity, proportion, and order (I, 257). The artist who wishes to create intrinsic beauty in his work must carefully imitate these qualities of natural beauty. In effect, Kames is encouraging the artist to aim for an organic unity in his work: "Hence it is required in every such work, that, like an organic system, it have its parts orderly arranged and mutually connected, bearing each of them a relation to the whole, some more intimate, some less, according to their destination" (I, 35). A work which possesses organic unity, therefore, has regularity and simplicity. Kames notes that, in the course of its history, art has degenerated from an emphasis on simplicity to an emphasis on ornament—on parts for their own sake rather than on parts for the whole.

Responsible criticism must, therefore, restore simplicity to all orders of art: "A literary performance intended merely for amusement, is suceptible of much ornament, as well as a music-room or a play-house; for in gaiety, the mind hath a peculiar relish for show and decoration. The most gorgeous apparel, however unsuitable to an actor in a regular tragedy, disgusts not at an opera. . . . On the other hand, a serious and important subject, admits not much ornament; nor a subject that of itself is extremely beautiful: and a subject that fills the mind with its loftiness and grandeur, appears best in a dress altogether plain" (II, 9-10).

Up to this point Kames has been speaking about beauty in single objects, but in Chapter X of *Elements*, "Congruity and

Propriety," he turns to the question of how a combination of objects or actions can be beautiful. Because two objects are beautiful in themselves, they will not necessarily produce an equal or greater beauty in combination: "... a thing beautiful in itself, may, with relation to other things, produce the strongest sense of incongruity" (II, 8). Congruity, therefore, is an emotional response to a pleasing association of objects or actions.[14] Since we always experience congruity in nature, art must imitate this pattern of association: "where the relation is strong and intimate, as betwixt a cause and its effect, a whole and its parts, we require that the things be suited to each other in the strictest manner: where the relation is slight, or accidental, as among things jumbled together in the same place, we demand little or no congruity" (II, 7).

Congruity explains in psychological terms the critical commonplace of decorum. Most neo-classical critics had insisted that the language, theme, characterization, and setting of a poem or play must work in harmony with one another, and that never, for example, should low language be put in the mouth of a king. Kames points out why the thoughts, words, and actions of a character must complement one another. Incongruity of any sort would fail to produce a lively impression in the audience or reader:

Nothing is more intimately related to a man, than his sentiments, words, and actions; and therefore we require here the strictest conformity. When we find what we thus require, we have a lively sense of propriety: when we find the contrary, our sense of impropriety is not less lively. Hence the universal distaste of affectation, which consists in making a shew of greater delicacy and refinement than is suited either to the character or circumstances of the person. Nothing shows worse in a story than impropriety of manners. (II, 12)

In addition to simplicity and congruity, beauty also implies limitation in an object and completeness in an action. The beautiful object must be able to be taken in by the eye at a single glance. Even the grand and the sublime, which transcend the requirements of simplicity and regularity, must possess this quality of limitation: "An unbounded prospect doth not long continue agreeable: we soon feel a slight uneasiness, which increases with the time we bestow upon the prospect" (I, 381n). A beautiful action is one worked out to a logical conclusion:

"Hence our uneasiness, when an interesting story is broke off in the middle, when a piece of music ends without a close" (I, 380–81).

VIII   *Modes of Esthetic Perception: Grandeur and Sublimity*

Beauty is a calm passion which excess of any sort can destroy. Thus, the term "beauty" can be used to describe only those natural or artistic objects and actions which possess simplicity, regularity, and moderate proportions. However, man does react pleasurably to objects and actions which exceed the limitations of beauty; and esthetics must also take these pleasurable responses into account. Most important among them is man's pleasure in natural objects of great size and great elevation. Kames treats these pleasures and the objects causing them in Chapter IV, "Grandeur and Sublimity."

The sublime is one of the most important topics of criticism in the eighteenth century. As Samuel Monk and others have pointed out, in the half century following Boileau's 1674 translation of the most significant document on the subject, Longinus' *Treatise on the Sublime,* the meaning of sublime changed from the rhetorical to the psychological, from a kind of style to a kind of feeling.[15] More and more attention was turned to the sources of these feelings in nature and to ways in which art could evoke the sublime in its audience.

Kames feels that size and elevation are the principal natural sources of the sublime. For clarity's sake, he calls the emotional response to size or magnitude "grandeur"; the response to elevation, "sublimity." Only objects of a great size have esthetic value, for small objects are esthetically neutral. Like beauty, grandeur and sublimity have an objective and a subjective meaning: "they generally signify the quality or circumstance in objects by which the emotions of grandeur and sublimity are produced; sometimes the emotions themselves" (I, 277).

Kames is on fairly secure psychological ground when he describes an emotional state different in degree and often in kind from that of beauty. But he is on much less secure ground when he attempts to describe certain physical reactions which accompany this emotional experience. The following is more of the amusingly naïve mechanism which we have noted earlier in this chapter: "A great object dilates the breast, and makes the spectator endeavour to enlarge his bulk; which is remarkable in persons, who, insensible of delicacy, give way to nature without reserve; in describing a great object, they naturally expand themselves by drawing in air with all their force. An elevated object produces a different expression: it makes the spectator stretch upward and stand a tiptoe" (I, 276–77).[16]

Ludicrous as this sort of causal equivalence may seem, it does occasionally take place, as Kames's quotation from *Henry V* demonstrates:

> This day is call'd the feast of Crispian.
> He that outlives this day, and comes safe home,
> Will stand a tiptoe when this day is nam'd,
> And rouse him at the name of Crispian. Act 4, Sc. 8 (I, 291)

In this quotation, of course, we have figurative rather than literal sublimity. Language, sentiment, and character of certain kinds produce an emotion identical with that produced by natural elevation.

The experience of magnitude and elevation is pleasurable only within certain limits. When these limits are exceeded, the experience becomes distracting or even painful: "... the strongest emotion of grandeur is raised by an object that can be taken in at one view; an object so immense as not to be comprehended but in parts, tends rather to distract than satisfy the mind" (I, 293). Kames notes that the same limitation applies to natural and figurative elevation.

To produce and sustain the emotion of sublimity, sentiment and character in a work of art must not exceed the capacity of the human mind. Thus, for example, the poet must exclude superior beings, actions, or qualities which would overextend the mind and cause pain rather than pleasurable sublimity. While the supernatural in poetry can momentarily please and engage sympathetic participation, man cannot sustain the intense sympathetic response which the supernatural object or action demands. Here, in psychological terms, is the old Augustan maxim: "The proper study of mankind is man." Milton, who fails to recognize the limitations of sublimity in his epic poems, ultimately loses his reader:

...we are undoubtedly susceptible of a greater elevation than can be inspired by human actions the most heroic and magnanimous; witness what we feel from Milton's description of superior beings: yet every man must be sensible of a more constant and pleasant elevation, when the history of his own species is the subject; he enjoys an elevation equal to that of the greatest hero, of an Alexander or a Caesar, of a Brutus or an Epaminondas; he accompanies these heroes in their sublimest sentiments and most hazardous exploits, with a magnanimity equal to theirs; and finds it no stretch to preserve the same tone of mind for hours together, without sinking. The case is by no means the same in describing the actions or qualities of superior beings: the reader's imagination cannot keep pace with that of the poet; the mind, unable to support itself in a strained elevation, falls as from a height; and the fall is immoderate like the elevation. (I, 294-95)

For the remainder of Chapter IV, Kames develops five ways in which the artist may achieve and maintain grandeur or sublimity in his work. First, the artist has an advantage over nature since he can select and arrange his material for esthetic effect. If his aim is to arouse grandeur or sublimity, he must keep the low and trivial out of his work, lest the mind of the audience be distracted from the heights. Kames gives several interesting examples of effective artistic selection. He illustrates first how Aristaeus mixes the low and elevated and "is at the same time full of verbal antitheses and low conceit, extremely improper in a scene of distress" (I, 302). Homer, on the other hand, selects only the great and the terrible and thus produces a uniformly sublime effect. Longinus testifies to this effect; first in Aristaeus, then in Homer.

> Ye pow'rs, what madness! how on ships so frail
> (Tremendous thought!) can thoughtless mortals sail?
> For stormy seas they quit the pleasing plain,
> Plant woods in waves and dwell amidst the main.
> Far o'er the deep (a trackless path) they go,
> And wander oceans in pursuit of wo.
> No ease their hearts, no rest their eyes can find,
> On heaven their looks, and on the waves their mind.
> Sunk are their spirits, while their arms they rear,
> And gods are wearied with their fruitless prayer.

[77]

Bursts as a wave that from the cloud impends,
And swell'd with tempests on the ship descends.
White are the decks with foam: the winds aloud
Howl o'er the masts, and sing through every shrowd.
Pale, trembling, tir'd, the sailors freeze with fears,
And instant death on every wave appears. (I, 301–2)

What applies to poetry applies equally to painting and gardening. In painting the "nobler parts" of the subject must be kept most in view and any lowness must be suppressed: ". . . the folds of the drapery must be few and large; . . . foreshortenings are bad, because they make the parts appear little; and . . . the muscles ought to be kept as entire as possible, without being divided into small sections" (I, 306–07). In gardening, the parterre must not be divided into many small sections but into a few grand sections.

Kames's second suggestion for producing the sublime in art is a stylistic one: avoid abstract and general terms. Only particularity can produce emotion. General terms may express thought in a concise manner, "but images, which are the life of poetry, cannot be raised in any perfection, otherwise than by introducing particular objects" (I, 307).

Third, Kames cautions the artist to work up to grandeur or sublimity gradually through a succession of images. A single sublime phrase in a passage will engage the emotions, but will not raise them to a sublime level. On the other hand, a succession of images, each more elevated than the one before it, raises the mind to grandeur by gradual stages:

I shall produce but one instance from Shakespear which sets a few objects before the eye, without much pomp of language: it works its effect, by representing these objects in a climax, raising the mind higher and higher till it feel the emotion of grandeur in perfection:

> The cloud-capt tow'rs, the gorgeous palaces,
> The solemn temples, the great globe itself,
> Yea all which it inherit, shall dissolve, etc.

The cloud-capt tow'rs produce an elevating emotion, heightened by the *gorgeous palaces;* and the mind is carried still higher and higher by the images that follow. Successive images, making thus stronger and stronger impressions, must elevate more than any single image can do. (I, 310–11)

[78]

Fourth, grandeur and sublimity do not depend as much upon regularity and order as does beauty. The power of the emotions makes the spectator overlook irregularity in both nature and in art. Kames notes that even slight irregularity in a small building is disagreeable, while the observer is not esthetically disturbed by irregularity in a large Gothic cathedral. And "... in an epic poem we pardon many negligences, which would be intolerable in a sonnet or epigram" (I, 312).

Fifth, Kames cautions artists to avoid the false sublime, which is another way of saying "maintain decorum." An artistic performance is always displeasing, Kames says, when there is incongruity between style and subject matter. Bombast, for example, is ridiculous rather than sublime; and Kames gives several examples of this particular kind of ineptitude. While modern criticism might describe the following outburst from Jonson's *Sejanus* as the unique passion of Apicata, Kames views it as an unpleasant distortion of the common nature of man:

> The mother,
> Th' expulsed Apicata, finds them there;
> Whom when she saw lie spread on the degrees,
> After a world of fury on herself,
> Tearing her hair, defacing of her face,
> Beating her breasts and womb, kneeling amaz'd,
> Crying to heav'n, then to them; at last
> Her drowned voice got up above her woes:
> And with such black and bitter execrations,
> (As might affright the gods, and force the sun
> Run backward to the east; nay, make the old
> Deformed chaos rise again t' o'erwhelm
> Them, us, and all the world), she fills the air,
> Upbraids the heavens with their partial dooms,
> Defies their tyrannous powers, and demands
> What she and those poor innocents have transgress'd
> That they must suffer such a share in vengeance. Act 5, Sc. LAST
> (I, 317–18)

Similarly, a naturally elevated subject must be described in elevated language. Otherwise the subject will not please. In the following passage from *Catiline,* the furies tremble and Apollo (the Sun) sweats; such low behavior violates the principle of decorum:

> The furies stood on hills
> Circling the place, and trembled to see men
> Do more than they: whilst Piety left the field,
> Griev'd for that side, that in so bad a cause
> They knew not what a crime their valour was.
> The Sun stood still, and was, behind the cloud
> The battle made, seen sweating to drive up
> His frighted horse, whom still the noise drove backward. Act 5 (I, 320)

IX *Modes of Esthetic Perception: Wonder*

In Chapter VI, Kames discusses pleasure caused by novelty—by the unexpected appearance of objects. Novelty can be both natural and artificial, and it produces an emotion Kames calls "wonder" or "surprise." The novel object or action produces initially a most intense pleasure; but, if novelty is all it has to offer, the pleasure soon fades. What was originally novel soon becomes customary, unlike things beautiful and sublime which evoke a more intense esthetic response with each successive experience of them. Kames questions the taste of those whose esthetic sensibility is limited to emotions caused by novelty. A man of taste, he declares, has long since outgrown this philistinism.

Custom and habit can influence esthetic perception as much as novelty, as Kames points out in Chapter XIV; while repeated exposure to a certain object or action can have the desirable effect of making tolerable what was originally disagreeable, more often such exposure weakens the esthetic response. Even worse, custom can make legitimate what is essentially unnatural. Thus, Kames declares, we have come to accept, for example, certain kinds of unnatural behavior in Greek drama simply because such behavior was customary in the Classical period. But nature must prevail over custom. Natural taste must object to human sacrifice in Euripides' *Iphigenia* and to unnatural love in his *Phaedra*. Kames's judgments about the Greeks are also linked to his theory about the progress of civilization, which he was to develop at greater length in *Sketches of the History of Man*. "Such imbecillity," he points out, "can never find grace

[80]

with a modern audience: it may indeed produce some compassion for a people afflicted with absurd terrors, similar to what is felt in perusing a description of the Hottentotes" (II, 119).

X *Resemblance and Contrast as Sources of Esthetic Pleasure*

Up to this point, Kames has been speculating about single objects and their effects. He proceeds in Chapter VIII to determine what kind of emotional response resemblance or contrast among objects produces. A proper combination of objects and actions can enliven an impression, just as their improper combination dulls the impression. Once again the evaluating principle is association.

Kames's general rule is that the artistic creation of resemblance and contrast must avoid two extremes. It must neither compare things that are identical, nor contrast things totally different from each other. Neither extreme will produce pleasure. Poets of a "just taste," Kames declares, "draw all their similies from things that in the main differ widely from the principal subject; and they never attempt a contrast but where the things have a common genus and a resemblance in the capital circumstances: place together a large and a small sized animal of the same species, the one will appear greater the other less, than when viewed separately: when we oppose beauty to deformity, each makes a greater figure by the comparison" (I, 366). And such is Iago's contrast of himself and Othello: "He hath a daily beauty in his life,/That makes me ugly." (I, 367), or Shakespeare's brilliant juxta-position of the warrior and the fop in Hotspur's speech in *1 Henry IV*, beginning "My liege I did deny no prisoners."

After making an interesting application of the principle of resemblance to art, in which he argues against photographic realism in sculpture—for complete resemblance would not increase esthetic response and would therefore be simply redundant, Kames turns to the importance of contrast for the fine arts:

The emotions raised by the fine arts, are generally too nearly related to make a figure by resemblance; and for that reason their succession ought to be regulated as much as possible by contrast. This holds confessedly in epic and dramatic compositions; and the

[81]

best writers, led perhaps by a good taste more than by reasoning, have generally aimed at this beauty. It holds equally in music: in the same cantata, all the variety of emotions that are within the power of music, may not only be indulged, but, to make the greatest figure, ought to be contrasted. In gardening there is an additional reason for the rule: the emotions raised by that art are at best so faint, that every artifice should be used to give them their utmost strength: a field may be laid out in grand, sweet, gay, neat, wild, melancholy scenes; and when these are viewed in succession, grandeur ought to be contrasted with neatness, regularity with wildness, and gaity with melancholy, so as that each emotion may succeed its opposite: nay it is an improvement to intermix in the succession, rude uncultivated spots as well as unbounded views, which in themselves are disagreeable, but in succession heighten the feeling of the agreeable objects; and we have nature for our guide, who in her most beautiful landscapes often intermixes rugged rocks, dirty marshes, and barren stony heaths. (I, 390–91)

Kames's insights into the possibilities of contrast for the fine arts represents one of his most persuasive contributions to esthetic theory.

XI *Uniformity and Variety*

Kames's ninth chapter, "Uniformity and Variety," presents little that is new; it is in the main a restatement of Francis Hutcheson's theory that the uniformity and variety found in nature must determine the optimum combination of these qualities in art. The best art is that which imitates nature. Though a balance between uniformity and variety is the theoretical ideal for art, Kames stresses that in fact the artist must emphasize variety; for it is far more difficult to achieve:

In works exposed continually to public view, variety ought to be studied. It is a rule accordingly in sculpture, to contrast the different limbs of a statue, in order to give it all the variety possible. Though the cone in a single view be more beautiful than the pyramid; yet a pyramidal steeple, because of its variety, is justly preferred. For the same reason, the oval in compositions is preferred before the circle; and painters, in copying buildings or any regular work, endeavour to give an air of variety by representing the subject in an angular view: we are pleased with the variety without losing sight of the regularity. In a landscape representing animals, those especially of the same kind, contrast ought to prevail: to draw one sleeping another awake, one sitting another in motion, one moving toward the spectator another from him, is the life of such a performance. (I, 420–21)

Kames concludes the chapter by distinguishing between artificial beauty and beauty in general. Where Kames takes issue with Hutcheson's definition of beauty as "uniformity amid variety," he points out that in many areas, such as mathematics with its theorems and figures, beauty means only uniformity with no suggestion of variety. A definition such as Hutcheson's applies only to situations where a number of objects in a group or in succession are involved.

XII *Ridicule and Its Methods*

In his next four chapters Kames discusses "Congruity and Propriety (Chapter X), "Dignity and Meanness" (Chapter XI), "Ridicule" (Chapter XII), and "Wit" (Chapter XIII). Congruity and its relation to decorum and beauty has been discussed earlier in this chapter. Kames elaborates on the need for decorum in artistic works dealing with human nature in Chapter XI. While impropriety in art is generally unintentional and weakens the over-all effect of the work, deliberate and successful use of impropriety is possible. Kames discusses two of these possibilities in Chapter XII, "Ridicule," and in Chapter XIII, "Wit." The two artistic modes have in common some sort of incongruity, usually between the subject and the manner of handling it. What distinguishes them is moral purpose. Wit has no moral purpose; it simply makes light of the subject, treating it in a ludicrous fashion. Ridicule, by various means, criticizes its subject.

In Chapter XII, Kames discusses several methods of ridicule. The most common method is burlesque, and here Kames means what we would call "high burlesque"—treating a trivial subject in a heroic manner for the purpose of moral contrast, as in Boileau's *Lutrin*. Using the principle of limitation, which should by now be familiar to the reader, Kames cautions against extremes in the burlesque, lest the audience be unable to comprehend the author. He offers Pope's *Rape of the Lock* as an example of proper impropriety, but he admits that most of that poem is simply amusing rather than critical.

Ridicule also often makes use of humor, irony, and parody. Kames defines humor as impropriety in a character, revealed either through another's observations about him or through his own words. Here are examples of each:

A true critic in the perusal of a book, is like a dog at a feast, whose thoughts and stomach are wholly set upon what the guests fling away, and consequently is apt to snarl most when there are fewest bones.

Tale of a Tub (II, 47-48)

Quickly: The young man is an honest man.
Caius: What shall de honest man do in my closet? dere is no honest man dat shall come in my closet.

Merry Wives of Windsor (II, 50)

Irony is used for purposes of ridicule when an author laughs "at a man under disguise, by appearing to praise or speak well of him" (II, 52). Kames defines parody as the imitation of a serious work for purposes of amusement or ridicule. Pope uses it both ways: in *The Rape of the Lock,* he imitates Achilles' oath in the *Iliad* to poke fun at the Baron's oath on the lock; he imitates the history of Agamemnon's scepter to describe Belinda's hairpin. But Pope can also parody to ridicule, as he does in the *Dunciad.*

XIII *Wit*

"Wit," Kames states at the beginning of Chapter XIII, "is a quality of certain thoughts and expressions: the term is never applied to an action or a passion, and as little to an external object" (II, 60). He distinguishes two kinds of wit: "in the thought and in the words or expression." The second is what we call pun or play on words, and Kames criticizes this "bastard sort of wit" (II, 63). Wit "in the thought" occurs when things resembling each other only faintly or not at all are brought together. In this example from the *Tale of a Tub,* the application of "toe" and "birch" have only a faint resemblance to each other; but the persona sees them as identical. " 'For there is not through

[84]

all nature, another so callous and insensible a member as the world's posteriors, whether you apply to it the toe or the birch' " (II, 64).

In wit where things not resembling each other at all are brought together, causes are introduced which "have no natural relation to the effects produced"; illogical reasoning is used; small things are equated with great; or things are joined which are opposite in appearance. None of these "unnatural combinations," as Kames calls them, should be found in a serious work. They can, however, delight in a humorous work. In the following examples from Samuel Butler's *Hudibras,* the first attributes the rotting away of a scabbard to the manliness of the sword within it; the second concludes that honor is lodged in man's posterior because a kick there hurts his honor—a case of an undistributed middle term in the syllogism:

> The trenchant blade, toledo trusty,
> For want of fighting was grown rusty,
> And ate into itself, for lack
> Of some body to hew and hack,
> The peaceful scabbard where it dwelt,
> The rancour of its edge had felt:
> For of the lower end two handful,
> It had devoured, 'twas so manful;
> And so much scorned to lurk in case,
> As if it durst not shew its face. Canto 1 (II, 66–7)

> But Hudibras gave him a twitch,
> As quick as lightning, in the breach,
> Just in the place where honour's lodg'd,
> As wise philosophers have judg'd;
> Because a kick in that part, more
> Hurts honour, than deep wounds before. Canto 3 (II, 70)

A third kind of "unnatural wit" is close to zeugma ("And sometimes Counsel take—and sometimes Tea"), except that the dissimilar objects are attached to different verbs, as in the following from the *Rape of the Lock:*

> One speaks the glory of the British Queen,
> And one describes a charming Indian screen. Canto 3 (II, 70)

[85]

Sir Roger de Coverley uses a fourth kind of "unnatural wit" when he speaks of the widow he loves by linking the sparkling of a precious stone to that of his rich acres: "That he would have given her a coal-pit to have kept her in clean linen; and that her finger should have sparkled with one hundred of his richest acres" (II, 71). This practice of illustration is very useful and should have been followed by more eighteenth-century critics, whose trademark is the vague generalization. Kames's point throughout this section is that verbal ambiguity tends to break down the sympathetic contract.

XIV The Mechanical Operation of the Spirit

At several points in this chapter, I have called attention to an extreme form of mechanism by means of which Kames often reduces his own valid critical principles to absurdity. He has insisted, for example, that sympathy produces external physical signs; that, when one responds to literal or figurative elevation, his feeling of grandeur can be recognized by another through similar physical signs. In Chapter XV, "External Signs of Emotions and Passions," Kames develops fully this mechanistic theory. What Kames tries to prove is that the communication of feeling from one person to another depends as much upon facial expression and physical gesture as it does upon language, and indeed that language is to some extent physical.

Before the reader dismisses Lord Kames at this point as hopelessly naïve, let me say that he was working in a rhetorical tradition with a long and distinguished history, a rhetorical tradition which was represented in eighteenth-century Britain by the so-called elocutionary movement. Delivery had always been an important part of Classical rhetoric where it was usually called *pronuntiatio* or *actio*. Cicero's discussion of *actio* in *De Oratore* reveals how close Kames is to the Classical tradition: "For nature has assigned to every emotion a particular look and tone of voice and bearing of its own; and the whole of a person's frame and every look on his face and utterance of his voice are like the strings of a harp, and sound according as they are struck by each successive emotion ... delivery is wholly the concern of the feelings, and these are mirrored by the face and expressed by the eyes."[17]

In an important article on the elocutionary movement in eighteenth-century England, Professor W. S. Howell points out the continuation of this Ciceronian tradition in the work of Michel Le Faucheur, Charles Gildon, and Edmund Curll.[18] Le Foucheur's book, entitled in the 1727 English translation *The Art of Speaking in Public: or an Essay on the Actions of an Orator; as to His Pronunciation and Gesture,* has two chapters which "discuss gesture first in general and then as it relates to the various parts of the body, particularly the head, face, eyes, and hands."[19] Le Brun's *Conférence ... sur l'expression général et particulière* (1698) presented a similar argument and even included drawings of faces wearing the various passions.[20]

Kames bases his theory of "natural language" on the common nature of man. "The natural signs of emotions, voluntary, and involuntary, being nearly the same in all men, form an universal language, which no distance of place, no difference of tribe, no diversity of tongue, can darken or render doubtful. Education, though of mighty influence, hath not power to vary or sophisticate, far less to destroy, their significa-tion ... the author of our nature, attentive to our wants, hath provided a passage to the heart, which never can be obstructed while our eye-sight remains entire" (II, 131–32). "Hope, fear, joy, grief, are display'd externally: the character of a man can be read in his face" (II, 120). Informing all of these ideas, of course, is the theory of sympathy; the external signs of emotion, he asserts, are specific ways in which one person can communi-cate emotionally with another.

Emotion may be communicated through a tone of voice. Kames states that some sounds are universally equivalent to a particular emotion: " ... thus the unpremeditated tones of ad-miration, are the same in all men; as also of compassion, resent-ment, and despair" (II, 123). But the usual external signs of passion are gestures:

... excessive joy is expressed by leaping, dancing, or some elevation of the body: excessive grief by sinking or depressing it: and pros-tration and kneeling have been employ'd by all nations and in all ages to signify profound veneration. ... Humility ... is expressed nat-urally by hanging the head; arrogance, by its elevation; and languor or despondence, by reclining it to one side. The expressions of the hands are manifold: by different attitudes and motions, they express desire, hope, fear; they assist us in promising, in inviting, in keeping one at a distance; they are made instruments of threatening, of supplication, of praise, and of horror; they are employ'd in approving, in refusing, in questioning; in showing our joy, our sorrow, our doubts, our regret, our admiration. (II, 124–26)

...pride...is always expressed by an erect posture, reverence by prostration, and sorrow by a dejected look. (II, 139)

XV   *"Negative Capability"*

The sixteenth chapter of *Elements of Criticism* has the rather innocuous title "Sentiments," but the title belies the chapter's importance. Instead of additional observations on the moral value of feeling, which we would expect from such a title, Kames actually presents a quite modern-sounding theory of "felt thought," a theory which insists that ideas in a work of art must proceed from feeling, that art must strive to avoid a destructive "dissociation of sensibility."[21] In the best art, Kames declares, writer and character become one. Kames here anticipates the insight that John Keats half a century later was to call "negative capability."

Kames's observations about the artistic process depend on the theory of naturalism which he has worked out in *Elements:* the best art is the best imitation of human nature. What makes this sixteenth chapter especially perceptive is that he focuses his attention almost entirely on one genre, the drama, and works out the implications of naturalism for the development of character. After defining "sentiment" and its relation to passion, Kames compares Shakespeare's plays to French drama in order to illustrate propriety of sentiment. He then turns to practical observation about true and false sentiment.

Simply stated, a sentiment is thought prompted by passion, as distinct from abstract thought. In the natural order, therefore, such a thought would have an intimate connection, even an observable connection, to the passion which caused it. Art—and here Kames limits himself to forms in which character is of central importance, to the epic and especially drama—must maintain this intimate connection between thought and passion if it is to achieve ideal presence, the illusion of reality which is its greatest perfection. To understand the connection between thought and passion in a character, the writer must become the character; he must feel passion in order to "represent it to the life" (II, 158). Most dramatists, says Kames, describe passion rather than express it; and their characters therefore declaim rather than feel: "Unhappy is the player of genius who acts a capital part in what may be termed a *descriptive tragedy:* after he has assumed the very passion that is to be represented, how must he be cramped in his action, when he is forc'd to utter, not the sentiments of the passion he feels, but a cold description in the language of a by-stander?" (II, 159).

It would be unproductive to push the Kames-Keats comparison too far. Keats, like all post-Kantian writers, had quite a different notion of the imagination and of creativity in art. But it is interesting that both Kames and Keats choose Shakespeare as the dramatist who most perfectly represents what Keats would call "negative capability" and what Kames calls "expression" rather than "description" in drama. Kames compares Shakespeare with Corneille to illustrate the difference. He quotes Lear's speech about filial ingratitude and Othello's reflections after he murders Desdemona as examples of thought properly linked to feeling. His reasons for judging that these speeches contain sentiments mirroring natural passion we will discuss in a moment.

French drama, unlike Shakespearean drama, is generally descriptive. Led by Corneille, French writers have cultivated style rather than sentiment. Such a manner makes it impossible to distinguish between characters. Nothing could be more ludicrous than a low character expressing a passion in the language of French tragedy; and yet, if the passion be common to all men, it should always be able to be expressed in the same way "... the same passion is by all men expressed nearly in the same manner" (II, 164n.). Kames's comments on Corneille's *Cinna* are especially pertinent:

In the tragedy of *Cinna,* Æmilia, after the conspiracy was discovered, having nothing in view but racks and death to herself and her lover, receives a pardon from Augustus, attended with the brightest circumstances of magnanimity and tenderness. This is a happy situation for representing the passions of surprise and gratitude in their different stages, which seem to be what follow. These passions, raised at once to the utmost pitch, being at first too big for utterance, must, for some moments, be expressed by violent gestures only: so soon as there is vent for words, the first expressions are naturally broken and interrupted: at last we ought to expect a tide of intermingled sentiments, occasioned by the fluctuation of the mind betwixt the two passions. Æmilia is made to behave in a very different manner: with extreme coolness she describes her own situation, as if she were merely a spectator; or rather the poet takes the talk off her hands. (II, 164–66)

In the second half of Chapter XVI, Kames gives practical methods for achieving proper sentiments in drama and some illustrations of various kinds of faulty sentiments. First, Kames points out, passion is not uniform; its chief characteristic is change. Effective characterization must show passion developing gradually—as in the following passage from *The Mourning Bride*—instead of keeping one monotonous tone:

> *Almeria.* How hast thou charm'd
> The wildness of the waves and rocks to this?
> That thus relenting they have giv'n thee back
> To earth, to light and life, to love and me? Act I, Sc. 7 (II, 168)

Second, to convince an audience that a character is caught up by a particular passion, the writer must at the very least avoid having him talk philosophically; and Kames again criticizes French drama for encouraging this contradiction between thought and feeling. Third, an impassioned person can be agitated by several passions at the same time; and his sentiments ought to reflct this agitation, as Othello's do in these lines:

> *Aemilia.* Oh! my good Lord, I would speak a word with you.
> *Othello.* Yes, 'tis Aemilia—By and by—She's dead.
> 'Tis like she comes to speak of Cassio's death;
> The noise was high—Ha, no more moving?
> Still as the grave. Shall she come in? were't good?
> I think she stirs again—No—what's the best?
> If she come in, she'll, sure, speak to my wife;
> My wife! my wife! What wife? I have no wife;
> Oh insupportable! oh heavy hour! Act 5, Sc. 7 (II, 174-75)

[90]

Kames's remarks about faulty sentiments simply amplify what has been pointed out in the above paragraph. There are some interesting illustrations, however, as when Kames criticizes Milton for writing sentiments which do not agree with passion. Kames objects to a speech of Satan which proposes to express his rage, but which ends with a figure of speech. Obviously, Kames declares, a man in a state of rage would never use figurative language. He opposes on principle what he calls "fanciful or finical sentiments." "Sentiments that degenerate into point or conceit, however they may amuse in an idle hour, can never be the offspring of any serious or important passion" (II, 187).

Lord Kames, who has a rather curious idea about the relation of thought to language, believes that they can be separated and discussed independently—that ideas can, in short, be separated from the language in which they have been expressed. In Chapter XVII, therefore, he discusses "Language of Passion" to complete the cycle of passion, sentiment, and language. To be persuasive, he declares, language must mirror both passion and sentiment. "Elevated sentiments require elevated language: tender sentiments ought to be clothed in words that are soft and flowing: when the mind is depressed with any passion, the sentiments must be expressed in words that are humble, not low" (II, 212). Shakespeare is praised as the master of effective passionate language. His soliloquies do not run smoothly; their broken cadences reflect the fluctuation or development of passion. Effective language depends not only on proper level of usage, but also on sound and rhythm:

To preserve the foregoing resemblance betwixt words and their meaning, the sentiments of active and hurrying passions ought to be dressed in words where syllables prevail that are pronounced short or fast; for these make an impression of hurry and precipitation. Emotions, on the other hand, that rest upon their objects, are best expressed by words where syllables prevail that are pronounced long or slow. A person affected with melancholy has a languid and slow train of perceptions: the expression best suited to this state of mind, is where words not only of long but of many syllables abound in the composition; and for that reason, nothing can be finer than the following passage:

In those deep solitudes, and awful cells,
Where heav'nly-pensive Contemplation dwells,
And ever-musing Melancholy reigns.

Pope, *Eloisa to Abelard*

To preserve the same resemblance, another circumstance is requisite, that the language, like the emotion, be rough or smooth, broken or uniform. Calm and sweet passions are best expressed by words that glide softly: surprise, fear, and other turbulent passions, require an expression both rough and broken. (II, 215–16)

With this discussion of sentiments, Kames concludes his treatment of psychology and art. The remainder of *Elements of Criticism* is concerned with the relationship between the artistic ideal of naturalism and proper style.

CHAPTER 4

Elements of Criticism: Style

CHAPTERS XVIII–XXIII in *Elements of Criticism* are generally concerned with style or rhetoric.[1] While the limitations of this book make impossible an extensive survey of the
rhetorical tradition and of Kames's place in it, Helen Randall's
general observation on the subject may be useful:[2]

Aristotle's *Rhetoric* appears to have made at first hand no mark at
all upon the rhetorical chapters [of *Elements*]; Demetrius and Quintilian contributed a little; Cicero, Dionysius of Halicarnassus, and
Longinus, on the other hand, were obviously Kames's favorites, and
with some good reason. For, each in his own way, these last three
defined the art of oratory in terms which he [Kames] must have
found peculiarly attractive: in Cicero, the effects of the art involve
the feelings of men and therefore the art itself must derive directly
from knowledge of all the first principles (including subtle emotional
relations) of the human mind; in Dionysius, the effects of oratory
are of a more distinctly aesthetic character ... while in Longinus, the
devices of style are given a richly suggestive psychological interpretation, implying a creative imagination alert both to the qualities of
genuine emotion and to the means by which they may be expressed
or evoked. Above all else, the recognition by these classical rhetoricians of the naturalistic basis of expressive devices—of an art rooted
in nature but still possessed of its character as art—played directly
into the main outlines of Kames's critical argument.[3]

Many of the principles Kames develops in these chapters are
taken from earlier naturalistic rhetorics. Thus "harmony of content and style" had been stressed by Horace, Demetrius, Longinus, and Quintilian; "climax in the 'composition' of words," by
Cicero and Demetrius; "the comparative virtues of natural and
inverted style," by Demetrius, Quintilian, and Longinus; "the
legitimate uses of certain figures, the function and importance of

vivid imagery," by all four rhetoricians. Kames's great contribution was the relation of these principles to a carefully worked out psychology of human nature.[4]

I *Language and Thought*

In these chapters Kames explores several problems of style or language in relationship to thought. The reader unfamiliar with developments in rhetoric in the Renaissance may find unnecessary Kames's insistence that language always be discussed in relation to thought. Such emphasis was necessary in the eighteenth century. While Classical theory had generally stressed the natural relation between logic and rhetoric, a sixteenth-century movement led by Peter Ramus had made fashionable the concept that style could be considered independent of thought, style being purely ornamental with no essential relation to thought. In theoretical terms, rhetoric could, indeed must, be kept separate from logic. A writer was free to work out, as Ramus and his followers did, an elaborate system of rhetorical devices whose effectiveness could be determined independent of meaning. Reaction to the Ramist school led to new efforts to synthesize logic and rhetoric, to make style a more organic part of creative utterance. This synthetic movement found its chief exponents among the Cartesian philosophers at Port-Royal in France. Kames, following the lead of the Cartesian school, argues that to be persuasive language must have a clear relation to thought. His criterion for excellence should be one familiar to the reader by now: liveliness in language can only be achieved when language is natural, when it closely resembles thought, just as thought to be persuasive must resemble feeling.

In Chapter XVIII, Kames considers beauty of language under four headings: "Beauty of Language With Respect to Sound," "Beauty of Language With Respect to Signification," "Beauty of Language From a Resemblance Betwixt Sound and Signification," and "Versification." The first three sections repeat for language the principles and applications Kames has already discussed in the chapter on sentiments. He feels, however, that the two must be kept separate since it is possible, though not desirable, to have beauty of language without beauty of thought and vice versa.

[*94*]

Kames's analysis of the beauty of language-sounds, independent of thought, seems naïve in this age of descriptive linguistics and computer analysis. But in the eighteenth century it was quite common to discuss the relative merit of languages, depending on their phonetic texture. Some languages could be described as smooth; others, as rough. When natives pronounce a language with difficulty, says Kames, that language must be inferior to a smooth one. The most pleasing vowels are those furthest removed from phonetic extremes. But ". . . the agreeableness of contrast in the rougher language, for which the great variety of sounds gives ample opportunity, must, even in an effeminate ear, prevail over the more uniform sounds of the smoother language" (II, 253). Contrast and balance ultimately determine whether single sounds, syllables, words, and sentences are pleasing.

Language, therefore, possesses its own beauties and can be pleasing independent of thought. The most pleasing language, however, as Kames points out in the second section of Chapter XVIII, closely resembles thought in both choice and arrangement of words. The ideal for any writer or speaker is the Cartesian one of clear and distinct ideas:

Language may be considered as the dress of thought; and where the one is not suited to the other, we are sensible of incongruity, in the same manner as where a judge is dressed like a fop, or a peasant like a man of quality. The intimate connection that words have with their meaning, requires that both be in the same tone: or, to express the thing more plainly, the impression made by the words ought as nearly as possible to resemble the impression made by the thought: the similar emotions mix sweetly in the mind, and augment the pleasure. On the other hand, where the impressions made by the thought and the words are dissimilar, they are forc'd into a sort of unnatural union, which is disagreeable. (II, 269)

Kames's application of this principle to the choice and arrangement of words is interesting. Conjunctions, for example, should only be used to tie together things naturally linked by association. Artificial associations do not please. This observation extends beyond conjunctions: ". . . when we have occasion to mention the intimate connection that the soul has with the body, the expression ought to be *the soul and body;* because the particle *the,* relative to both, makes a connection in the expression, which resembles in some degree the connection in the thought: but when the soul is distinguished from the body, it is better to say *the soul and the body,* because the disjunction in the words resembles the disjunction in the thought" (II, 270–71). In comparisons, moreover, resembling objects should be described in resembling words.

As for the arrangement of words, perspicuity remains the ideal. Kames realizes that an absolutely "natural style"—one in which subject, predicate, and object appear in order—could become boring. Inversion contributes to the beauty of language if it does not interfere with clarity: "... inversion is susceptible of many beauties that are totally excluded in a natural arrangement of words. From these premises it clearly follows, that inversion ought not to be indulged, unless in order to reach some beauty superior to that of a natural style. It may with great certainty be pronounced, that every inversion which is not governed by this rule, will appear harsh and strained" (II, 346–47). Furthermore, words "expressing things connected in the thought, ought to be placed as near together as possible" (II, 320).

Finally Kames defends the excellence of the periodic style on psychological grounds. In presenting a group of objects, the writer achieves greatest effect when the most impressive object is placed last, so that the mind may gradually ascend to it. Therefore, "That order of words in a period will always be the most agreeable, where, without obscuring the sense, the most important images, the most sonorous words, and the longest members, bring up the rear" (II, 334).

In the third section of Chapter XVIII, Kames considers how the sounds of language imitate thought. He distinguishes between pure onomatopoeia, or the use of words which truly sound like what they signify, and mimetic language, which only resembles what it describes. Few English words, Kames declares, are onomatopoetic. Yet effective speech and writing make frequent use of mimetic language: "... witness the word *running,* composed of two short syllables; and more remarkably the words *rapidity, impetuosity, precipitation.* Brutal manners produce in the spectator, an emotion not unlike what is produced by a harsh and rough sound; and hence the beauty of the figurative expression, *rugged* manners. Again, the word *little,* being pronounced with a very small aperture of the mouth, has a weak and faint sound, which makes an impression resembling that made by any diminutive object" (II, 353). Kames includes several other interesting examples of mimetic language. Rough sounds in succession resemble rough motion; smooth sounds resemble gentle motion:

> Two craggy rocks projecting to the main,
> The roaring wind's tempestuous rage restrain;
> Within, the waves in softer murmurs glide,
> And ships secure without their haulsers ride.
>
> *Odyssey,* iii (II, 356)

> Soft is the strain when Zephyr gently blows
> And the smooth stream in smoother numbers flows.
>
> *Essay on Criticism* (II, 357)

Slowly pronounced polysyllables resemble the feeling of melancholy:

> In those deep solitudes and awful cells,
> Where heavn'ly-pensive Contemplation dwells,
> And ever-musing Melancholy reigns.
>
> *Eloisa and Abelard* (II, 358)

II *Versification: The Heroic Couplet and Blank Verse*

In the final section of Chapter XVIII, Lord Kames turns to the esthetics of versification, limiting his discussion to three verse forms: Latin hexameter, the heroic couplet, and blank verse. The heroic couplet was the most popular verse form in the eighteenth century, and Kames's analysis of it is the fullest technical criticism of the form that I know of in the eighteenth-century. He begins the general subject of versification by distinguishing verse from prose. Verse, he says, is more artfully ordered than prose; it can achieve a uniformity and a variety which produce a distinctive pleasure in the sensitive audience. The peculiar pleasure of verse comes from its modulation, which is more perfect than that of prose. Modulation, as Kames uses the term, means succession of long and short syllables, high and low pitches in a line. His discussion of the three verse forms develops around five structural elements: first, the number of syllables composing a line; second, the different lengths of the syllables; third, the arrangement of these syllables combined in words; fourth, the use of pause or stop in the line; fifth, accent or pitch (II, 375).

Kames's remarks about the Latin hexameter line reveal an interesting application of his criterion of naturalism. The Latin verse form, he declares, is governed by rules so inflexible as to make the line unnatural; but these rules are necessary to preserve the melody of the line. He states, for example, that all hexameter lines must take the same time to read and that the variation from twelve to twenty-four syllables must be compensated for by a greater or lesser number of feet. As for pause and accent, the hexameter line must always end with a full stop and must always have a pause after the fifth or sixth syllable. In every line one syllable must be distinguishable from the rest by a strong accent. Ideally, rules for versification should allow sound to follow sense. The Latin hexameter line lacks sufficient possibilities for variation and makes this ideal impossible to achieve:

An Hexameter line, to preserve its melody, cannot well admit any greater relaxation; and yet in a narrative poem, it is extremely difficult to adhere strictly to the rule even with these indulgences. Virgil, the greatest poet for versification that ever existed, is forc'd often to end a line without any close in the sense, and as often to close the sense during the running of a line: though a close in the melody during the movement of the thought, or a close in the thought during the movement of the melody, cannot fail to be disagreeable. (II, 390–91)

In most cases Kames is aware that esthetic theory must yield to practice. His inflexible commitment to a particular theory of Latin scansion, however, blinds him to the real prosodic excellence of Virgil's poetry.

Kames does not find this incongruity between versification and naturalism in English heroic verse because of its greater possibilities for variety. He discusses first the couplet, then blank verse, although many of his observations could be applied to either form. The usual line has ten syllables, five long and five short. Occasionally, the line may be extended to eleven syllables by the addition of a short and long syllable to the second line of the couplet; this longer line is called an "Alexandrine":

A needless Alexandrine ends the song,
That, like a wounded snake, drags its slow length along. (II, 398)

English verse differs from Latin verse in quantity, "the relative length of time required to utter a syllable."[5] The length of the Latin syllable is fixed, whereas the length of the English syllable depends more on the accent of the word in which it occurs. Therefore, no rule can be made for quantity in English verse.

When Kames turns to the arrangement of the heroic line, he makes the rather curious assertion that the only variation permitted in the iambic pentameter line is an initial trochaic foot. All other internal inversions and variations he regards as imperfections. Kames certainly seems to be unduly restrictive here, violating his own principle of naturalism. It is difficult to understand how the form of the iambic line suffers from other internal variations. The restriction seems especially strange when compared to the full discussion of the use of pause in the line. Thus, the following line from Pope is imperfect: "This nymph, to the destruction of mankind." Kames reasons that the poet has given a "false quantity" to the word "the" which is always short. The modern reader would, I suppose, say that the line begins with a spondee (two long syllables), followed by a pyrrhic (two short syllables). Kames is unwilling to allow this kind of variation. Such a restrictive theory of "arrangement" also makes impossible the pleasurable use of certain polysyllabic words which in themselves have a pleasing melody, words like "magnanimity," "impetuosity," and "ornamental." Kames feels that the use of such words flaws the following lines because the regular flow of iambic feet is broken:

And old impertinence//expel by new.

Love in these labyrinths//his slaves detains.

Her eyes half-languishing//half drown'd in tears. (II, 402)

The heroic line can have two kinds of pause which Kames calls "capital pause" and "semi-pause." The capital pause comes toward the middle of the line and may occur after the fourth, fifth, sixth, or seventh syllable. Kames uses the position of the capital pause as a means of distinguishing the four orders of the heroic line, discussed below. There are commonly two semi-pauses in each line coming before and after the capital pause, the first usually after the first long syllable and the second after the sixth, seventh, or eighth syllable. While it is obvious from these rules that Kames makes the heroic line somewhat inflexible, his principle of naturalism remains relevant, as it does not for his discussion of Latin hexameter. Pause, for instance, should never divide a word, as it does in the following line: "A noble super//fluity it craves." This line is flawed because, according to Kames's system, the capital pause cannot occur after the seventh syllable.

Moreover, pause should never come between an adjective and the noun it modifies, as in the following line: "Of thousand//bright inhabitants of air." While the modern reader would place the capital pause in this line after the eighth syllable, Kames maintains that doing so is against the rules. Pause may, however, occur between the adjective and noun if the adjective comes after the noun, since an object may be conceived apart from its qualities: "And curs'd with hearts//unknowing how to yield." He goes on, essentially along the lines described above, to point out the relationship of the various other parts of speech—verb and adverb, subject and verb—to the capital pause. The concluding pause in a line should be as strong as that of the capital pause. And the concluding pause of a couplet should be accompanied by a similar pause in meaning.

As for accent, the normal pattern for the heroic line is five accented syllables. The principal accent in the line should come just before the capital pause, though in some lines a short syllable may intervene before this pause. The sense of the verse should parallel the accent pattern so that an important word will occur where there is a primary accent.

English heroic verse has four orders or modes, depending on the position of the capital pause. In the first order, the pause occurs after the fourth syllable: "Belinda smil'd//and all the world was gay." Lines of the second order have the capital pause after the fifth syllable: "And all the trophies//of his former lover." The third order has the pause after the sixth syllable: "To fifty chosen sylphs,//of special note/We trust the important charge,//the petticoat." In the fourth order the capital pause comes after the seventh syllable: "And hew triumphal arches//to the ground." Kames makes some interesting observations on the particular beauty of these four orders:

A line of the first order is of all the most spirited and lively. To produce this effect, several of the circumstances above mentioned concur: the accent, being followed instantly by a pause, makes an illustrious figure: the elevated tone of the accent elevates the mind: the mind is supported in its elevation by the sudden unprepared pause which rouses and animates: and the line itself, representing by its unequal division an ascending series, carries the mind still higher, making an impression similar to that of mounting upward. The second order has a modulation sensibly sweet, soft, and flowing: the accent is not so sprightly as in the former, because a short syllable intervenes betwixt it and the pause: its elevation, by the same means, vanisheth instantaneously: the mind, by a falling voice, is gently prepared for a stop: and the pleasure of uniformity from division of the line into two equal parts, is calm and sweet. The third order has a modulation not so easily expressed in words: it in part resembles the first order, by the liveliness of an accent succeeded instantly by a full pause: but then the elevation occasioned by this circumstance, is balanced in some degree by the remitted effort in pronouncing the second portion, which remitted effort has a tendency to rest. Another circumstance distinguisheth it remarkably: its capital accent comes late, being placed on the sixth syllable; and this circumstance bestows on it an air of gravity and solemnity. The last order resembles the second in the mildness of its accent and softness of its pause: it is still more solemn than the third, by the lateness of its capital accent: it also possesses in a higher degree than the third, the tendency to rest; and by that circumstance is of all the best qualified for closing a period in the completest manner. (II, 440-42)

He concludes by speculating on the ways in which various combinations of these orders will please. It might be objected that this is overly refined estheticism, but I think that Kames has offered some practical insights into the craftsmanship of this poetic form.

While recognizing the intrinsic melodic value of rhyme in the couplet, Kames suggests that any poetic form requiring its constant use is limited in terms of the subjects and emotions it can naturally express. "We find that [rhyme] rouses the mind, and produceth an emotion moderately gay without dignity or elevation: like the murmuring of a brook gliding through pebbles, it calms the mind when perturbed, and gently raises it when sunk" (II, 466). But rhyme does not allow verse to accompany the imagination "in its boldest flights" (II, 452). Similarly, requiring a pause in meaning at the end of a closed couplet either restricts the expressive possibilities of the verse or forces the poet into unnaturalness. Kames is suggesting, of course, that for many subjects—especially for "serious subjects," like epic and tragedy—the rhymed couplet is an unnatural form. Blank verse would be a much more suitable vehicle. The discussion is interesting in light of the movement away from the heroic couplet and toward blank verse in the later eighteenth century; more and more, poets felt the need to write verse paragraphs instead of two-line epigrams. They sought a form which would be a truer reflection of their sensibilities, and such a search for form was to become a dominant characteristic of the Romantic movement.

Kames concludes his discussion of the beauty of language with a section on meter in which he distinguishes some thirty-four kinds of metrical feet of which twenty pertain to English verse. In addition to the usual run from iamb to dactyl, Kames includes some intriguing types. Thus the "proceleusmaticus" foot has four short syllables ("necessary"); "antipastus," two long syllables between two short syllables ("Alexander"); the second type of "paeon" foot, a second long syllable and three others which are short ("rapidity"). Such observations also give the reader some notions about eighteenth-century pronunciation.

III *Simile and Metaphor*

Kames has insisted up to this point that in any literary work style must work in support of nature. The principle holds true for the use of comparisons, which he takes up in Chapter XIX. To be natural, and thus to be pleasing, a comparison must be purposeful; and Kames distinguishes five ways in which a comparison can please: first, by drawing attention to some "unusual resemblance or contrast"; second, by "setting an object in the strongest light"; third, by associating an object with something else that is pleasurable; fourth, by "elevating an object"; and fifth, by "depressing it" (III, 3–4). Not only must comparison be purposeful, it must also be clear; and Kames demands the same kind of clarity he has insisted on in language used literally. Thus, the two things compared must be similar; indeed, he goes on, it is difficult to imagine a successful comparison in which objects of different senses are compared. And, when an abstraction is the subject of a comparison, the abstraction must be imagined to be a living thing, as when Shakespeare compares adversity to a toad and slander to the bite of a crocodile. Successful metaphor, according to Kames, depends on a similarity in the emotional effect produced by two objects. Here again is the familiar principle of association:

There is no resemblance betwixt a flower-pot and a chearful song; and yet they may be compared with respect to their effects, the emotions they produce in the mind being extremely similar. There is as little resemblance betwixt fraternal concord and precious ointment; and yet observe how successfully they are compared with respect to the impressions they make:

> Behold, how good and pleasant it is for brethren
> to dwell together in unity. It is like the precious
> ointment upon the head, that ran down upon Aaron's
> beard, and descended to the skirts of his garment.
> *Psalm 133* (III, 9)

Kames then illustrates the five methods of comparison. There is, first of all, comparison through an unusual resemblance or contrast, one which is not immediately apparent to the audience and which therefore must be developed by the poet to be understood. Such a comparison borders on the unnatural, and a poet's failure to elucidate the resemblance or contrast could flaw the comparison. Kames seems to be talking here about what later came to be known as a "conceit," a kind of comparison which Samuel Johnson summarily rejected as unnatural in poetry. Kames is more tolerant of unusual comparisons, pro vided that, like the following example from *As You Like It,* the resemblance is clearly worked out:

> Sweet are the uses of Adversity,
> Which, like the toad, ugly and venomous,
> Wears yet a precious jewel in her head. ACT 2, Sc. 1 (III, 11)

Illustration, the second method of comparison, does not involve an unusual resemblance or contrast; for resemblance between the two things compared is immediately apparent. Illustration places the principal object "in its strongest light," as Kames puts it. The comparison in the following passage from *Macbeth* is an illustration. Since the relationship between life and a walking player is much less obscure than that between adversity and a toad, Shakespeare need not have elaborated the comparison:

> Out, out, brief candle!
> Life's but a walking shadow, a poor player,
> That struts and frets his hour upon the stage,
> And then is heard no more. ACT 5, Sc. 5 (III, 17-18)

While illustration seeks simply to clarify the principal object, the other three methods of comparison which Kames distinguishes seek to change the audience's attitude toward the principal object. Milton, using the third method of comparison, seeks to embellish the principal object "by associating it with others that are agreeable" (III, 21):

> He scarce had ceas'd, when the superior fiend
> Was moving toward the shore; his pond'rous shield,
> Ethereal temper, massy, large, and round,
> Behind him cast; the broad circumference
> Hung on his shoulders like the moon, whose orb
> Through optic glass the Tuscan artist views
> At ev'ning from the top of Fesole,
> Or in Valdarno, to descry new lands,
> Rivers, or mountains, in her spotty globe. BOOK 1 (III, 21-22)

Comparisons also can elevate or depress the principal object. This quotation from *Richard III,* which Kames gives as an example of the fourth method, allegedly uplifts the principle object by associating it with a high elevation:

[104]

> Methinks, King Richard and myself should meet
> With no less terror than the elements
> Of fire and water, when their thund'ring shock,
> At meeting tears the cloudy cheeks of heaven. Act 3, Sc. 5 (III, 25)

Kames says that Homer, using the fifth and final method of comparison, lowers the principal object by comparing the shouts of the Trojans to the noise of cranes and to the bleating of sheep, and contrasts this cacophony with the silent march of the Greeks (III, 29).

Language used for comparison, as for any other purpose, must fit the psychological situation in which it occurs. Only a man in an agitated state of mind would use comparisons, says Kames, and therefore only in these dramatic situations should they be introduced: "... similies are not the language of a man in his ordinary state of mind, dispatching his daily and usual work" (III, 33). Kames quotes Longinus: ". . . the proper time for metaphor, is when the passions are so swelled as to hurry on like a torrent" (III, 31n). If comparisons are improper or unnatural when the mind is calm, they are equally unnatural when the agitation of the mind is extreme. Kames includes several examples of comparisons which have no relation to the psychological state of the speaker. Thus the gardener in *Richard II* is too calm to indulge in the elaborate comparison between "dangling apricocks" and "unruly children," as Shakespeare has him do. On the other hand, Rutland, under threat of death in *3 Henry VI,* could never have used the metaphoric language Shakespeare gives him.

Kames concludes Chapter XIX with a discussion of what he calls "purely verbal comparisons"—comparisons which, though proper to the psychological situation in which they occur, are nevertheless unnatural. Such comparisons suggest a relationship between two objects which is not literally true. Thus, in modern English it would be unnatural to refer to someone as a "hot-head" because his head is not in fact physically hot. Kames seems unable to grasp the central power of metaphor to provide insights about the principal object by transferring to it qualities which may not be literally true. The following passage from *Coriolanus,* Kames declares has an imperfect comparison:

> The noble sister of Poplicola,
> The moon of Rome; chaste as the isicle
> That's curdled by the frost from purest snow,
> And hangs on Dian's temple. ACT 5, SC. 3 (III, 49)

Now, of course, Valeria is not cold to the touch; but, by thinking about her chastity as an icicle, we learn much about her character which a literal comparison such as "chaste as Diana" would not communicate. Such coldness, for instance, gives us an idea of her physical appearance, of her tone of voice, perhaps even of her actions.

Kames also finds these lines from Pope's *Essay on Man* similarly flawed: "And hence one master passion in the breast,/Like Aaron's serpent, swallows up the rest" (III, 52). And yet, if a master passion does not literally swallow up other passions within a man, surely thinking about its operation in this way reveals much about its voraciousness which a literal comparison would not reveal. Fortunately for English poetry, Kames's restrictions on comparison had little practical effect.

IV *Figures of Speech*

Kames's discussion of figures of speech, a traditional part of rhetoric, has an historical importance since it reflects the dominant eighteenth-century attitude toward the subject. He also has some interesting things to say about the relationship between psychology and particular figures of speech. But we must first of all understand what a "figure of speech" means to Kames. According to most Classical and Renaissance writers, rhetoric was one of the three kinds of communication among men. It was distinguished from the other two, logic and poetics, by its end, communication between the learned and the vulgar. Logic concerned itself with communication among the learned; poetics, with a combination of both.[6] A major theoretical revolution occurred in the mid-sixteenth century, as was pointed out earlier in this chapter, when Ramus redefined logic and rhetoric, arguing that logic and rhetoric were both part of every deliberate human communication. Logic accounted for the invention and arrangement of the ideas; rhetoric, for the style and delivery. Ramus' theory was extremely influential. For the next hundred years or so, rhetoric became the science of ornamenting ideas, a science highly refined in the late sixteenth and seventeenth centuries in England.

Figures of speech have traditionally been considered part of rhetoric. Classical writers like Quintilian spoke of two general classes of words, "tropes" and "figures." Sometimes, for clarity, the term "schemes" was used for figures. Scheme or figure is a way of describing the shape of a word or a sentence, and of describing various possible changes in these shapes. Thus parallelism would be a scheme. A word becomes a trope when it is used with some sort of transferred meaning, as in metaphor or metonymy.[7] When rhetoric was divorced from logic by Ramus and his followers, schemes, figures, and even tropes began to be discussed apart from meaning and in terms of their stylistic excellence rather than in terms of their dramatic or psychological propriety.

Kames and other eighteenth-century rhetoricians like George Campbell and Hugh Blair, who rejected this artificial separation of logic and rhetoric,[8] insisted that some tropes and certain kinds of figures were by definition part of meaning. As Campbell puts it: "It hath been common with rhetoricians to rank under the article of diction, not only all the tropes, but even the greater part of the figures of eloquence, which they have uniformly considered as qualities or ornaments merely of elocution, and therefore as what ought to be explained among the properties of style. It is however certain, that some of them have a closer connection with the thought than with the expression."[9] Campbell then restates the traditional distinction of Quintilian between figures of thought and figures of style. A figure of thought refers to the literal meaning of a word; a figure of style, to its shape. Kames, who makes the same distinction, insists that figures of thought be subject to the same requirements of naturalism as any other use of language.

Kames gives most attention in the chapter to three tropes: personification, metaphor, and allegory. He also discusses apostrophe, hyperbole, and metonymy. Personification, like all strategies of language, must be psychologically justified: "... the mind is prone to bestow sensibility upon things inanimate, where that violent effect is necessary to gratify passion"

(III, 62). When a passion becomes excessive, "it is not to be gratified but by sympathy from others; and if denied that consolation in a natural way, it will even convert things inanimate into sympathising beings" (III, 64). Kames calls the use of tropes which conform to psychological naturalism "passionate"; those which do not, "descriptive." In the two following passages from *Julius Caesar* and *Hamlet,* the first contains a passionate personification; the second a descriptive one. Mark Antony's emotional state would naturally lead to such a use of language; Horatio's would not:

> O pardon me, thou bleeding piece of earth,
> That I am meek and gentle with these butchers.
> Thou art the ruins of the noblest man
> That ever lived in the tide of times. ACT 3, SC. 4 (III, 62)

> But look, the morn, in russet mantle clad,
> Walks o'er the dew of yon high eastward hill. ACT 1, SC. 1 (III, 70)

Kames cautions the writer that the state of passion which leads to personification is of short duration; therefore, an extended personification soon becomes unnatural. The writer must also take care not to make the human activities of the thing personified too farfetched, as does Shakespeare when he makes the winds enamored of the sails on Cleopatra's barge (III, 89-90).

In Section VI of Chapter XX, Kames turns to the tropes of metaphor, simile, and allegory. Unlike modern critics who view simile and metaphor as two distinct ways of describing a relation between things, he asserts they are the same, distinguished only by mode of expression, not by thought:

A metaphor differs from a simile, in form only, not in substance. In a simile the two different subjects are kept distinct in the expression, as well as in the thought: in a metaphor, the two subjects are kept distinct in thought only, not in expression. A hero resembles a lion, and upon that resemblance many similes have been made by Homer and other poets. But instead of resembling a lion, let us take the aid of the imagination, and feign or figure the hero to be a lion: by this variation the simile is converted into a metaphor. (III, 122)

Metaphor is distinguished from allegory by the operation of its tenor and vehicle. The *"vehicle* is the figure that carries the weight of the comparison, while the *tenor* is the subject to which the vehicle refers."[10] In metaphor both tenor and vehicle are expressed. When Tennyson describes an eagle, both the eagle and the human abilities with which its actions are compared appear: "He clasps the crag with crooked hands." In allegory, according to Kames, only the vehicle is expressed; the tenor is implied, as in the following Psalm when the vineyard stands for God's chosen people, although there is no explicit reference to the Jews in the passage:

Thou hast brought a vine out of Egypt: thou hast cast out the heathen, and planted it. Thou didst cause it to take deep root, and it filled the land. The hills were covered with its shadow, and the boughs thereof were like the goodly cedars. Why hast thou then broken down her hedges, so that all which pass do pluck her? The boar out of the wood doth waste it, and the wild beast doth devour it. Return, we beseech thee, O God of hosts: look down from heaven, and behold, and visit this vine, and the vineyard thy right hand hath planted, and the branch thou madest strong for thyself. (III, 127–28)

Kames's rules for the effective use of metaphor and allegory repeat in large part those he suggests in his chapter on comparison. Thus the resemblance between tenor and vehicle must be neither too strong nor too faint. The level of usage on both sides of the comparison must be similar or the effect is burlesque. The writer must avoid the complications of mixed metaphor since clarity is his central purpose. And neither metaphor nor allegory should be extended. Extended metaphor, Kames maintains, soon tires the mind. His illustration of this sort of imperfection fits in with the age's general distrust of the allegorical temper: "For the same reason, however agreeable at first long allegories may be by their novelty, they never afford any lasting pleasure: witness the *Fairy Queen,* which with great power of expression, variety of images, and melody of versification, is scarce ever read a second time" (III 136).

Kames entitles the final section of Chapter XX "Figure of Speech," and in it he discusses the ways in which tropes can also be figures. The words used can ornament as well as illuminate. "Morning of life," he says illustrates this dual purpose. The principal meaning is "youth," but Kames points out that the word "morning" has certain beauties which are additional to those transferred to an understanding of "youth." Kames would deny, I suppose, the notion that metaphor involves the complete identification of one thing with another, although in another place in the chapter he has implied that such is not the case.[11] At any rate, since these additional beauties belong to the meaning of "morning" rather than to its shape, the word is a figure of thought rather than a figure of style.[12]

V *Epic and Drama: Rules and Reason*

The next two chapters of *Elements of Criticism*—Chapter XXI, "Narration and Description," and Chapter XXII, "Epic and Dramatic Compositions"—reassert the ideal of psychological naturalism which Kames has been stressing throughout the book. Language must function as the mirror of feeling and of thought. Since figurative language in a work should indicate a degree of passion in the speaker, such language should be avoided in an essentially dispassionate work like history. And only occasional use should be made of it in epic poetry which is essentially historical. Addressing himself once again to the problem of the general and the particular in language, Kames notes the importance of particular detail in all narration and description, but especially in the development of character, to produce in the reader the liveliness necessary for belief. Here again is Kames's theory of ideal presence.

In Chapter XXIII, Kames discusses various rules for the epic and for tragedy. He insists that in an epic poem all episodes be related to the central action, and he criticizes irrelevant digressions in Homer and Milton. Since his criterion for excellence in art is always naturalism, he disapproves of "epic machinery," or the introduction of supernatural beings as real people. Kames adopts Aristotle's notion of the tragic hero: the imperfect man who wills his own destruction through some action, the end of which he has not foreseen. He concludes this fairly conventional chapter by voicing his disapproval of the double plot in tragedy and of violence presented on stage. The subplot distracts the mind from the critical action and threatens the sympathetic contract between actor and audience. On-stage violence carries the emotional reaction of the audience beyond the bounds of art.

Kames's most interesting contribution to the theory of the drama comes in Chapter XXIII, "The Three Unities." Readers familiar with the history of criticism will recognize the "Aristotelian problem" which found its way into virtually every critical treatise from the Italian Renaissance to the eighteenth century. Aristotle, so these critics claimed, had insisted that tragedy must have unity of time, place, and action. Italian critics such as Scaliger and Castelvetro had refined this requirement to mean that the dramatic action could not involve a longer period of time than it took for the performance of the play, and that a single setting must serve for the entire play. In this chapter of *Elements*, Kames quite successfully refutes such hypernaturalism with common sense. Samuel Johnson is usually given credit for questioning the authority of the three unities in his "Preface to Shakespeare," but *Elements of Criticism* appeared three years before Johnson's essay.

As Kames points out, the traditional interpretation of Aristotle must yield to the text of the *Poetics*. Aristotle there makes no precise rules about unity of time and place in tragedy; he insists only on the unity of action. Plot, he says, must have "a length which allows of the hero passing by a series of probable or necessary stages from misfortune to happiness or from happiness to misfortune."[13] He suggests that this is usually "within a single circuit of the sun,"[14] but he does not make this part of his definition of tragedy. What is essential is that "the story ... represent one action, a complete whole, with its several incidents so clearly connected that the transferral or withdrawal of any one of them will disjoin and dislocate the whole."[15]

The principle of unity of action must be accepted, as Kames has observed several times before in other contexts, because it is so intimately connected with natural association, especially with the relation of cause and effect. The mind receives its greatest pleasure from observing a train of events. Plot often also involves the overcoming of obstruction, which intensifies the viewer's pleasure. Comparisons between the *Aeneid* and the

Iliad illustrate this theory. The *Iliad* must finally be judged inferior to the *Aeneid* because its unity of action is not so clear as that of the Latin poem:

In the *Aeneid,* the hero, after many obstructions, brings his plan to perfection. The *Iliad* is formed upon a different model: it begins with a quarrel betwixt Achilles and Agamemnon; goes on to describe the several effects produced by that cause; and ends in a reconciliation. Here is unity of action, no doubt, a beginning, a middle, and an end; but inferior to that of the *Aeneid:* which will thus appear. The mind hath a propensity to go forward in the chain of history: it keeps always in view the expected event; and when the incidents or underparts are connected together by their relation to the event, the mind runs sweetly and easily along them. This pleasure we have in the *Aeneid.* It is not altogether so pleasant, as in the *Iliad,* to connect effects by their common cause; for such connection forces the mind to a continual retrospect: looking backward is like walking backward. (III, 292–93)

While unity of action, therefore, has a foundation in nature, the unities of time and place do not. Kames makes the excellent historical observation that Greek drama was forced to follow these two unities because one of its essential parts was choral singing. Since the chorus never left the stage, the unities of time and place had to be preserved:

All authors agree, that tragedy in Greece, was derived from the hymns in praise of Bacchus, which were sung in parts by a chorus. Thespis, to relieve the singers, and for the sake of variety, introduced one actor; whose province it was to explain historically the subject of the song, and who occasionally represented one or other personage. Eschylus, introducing a second actor, formed the dialogue; by which the performance became dramatic: and the actors were multiplied where the subject represented made it necessary. But still, the chorus, which gave a beginning to tragedy, was considered as an essential part of its constitution. (III, 301)

Kames remarks later in the chapter that the Greeks were forced into some unnatural situations as a result of the prescribed unities:

Alcestes, in *Euripides,* at the point of death, is brought from the palace to the place of action, groaning, and lamenting her untimely fate. In the *Trachiniens* of Sophocles, a secret is imparted to Dejanira, the wife of Hercules, in presence of the chorus. In the tragedy of *Iphigenia,* the messenger employ'd to carry Clitemnestra the news that Iphigenia was sacrificed, stops short at the place of action, and with a loud voice calls the Queen from her palace to hear the news. Again, in the *Iphigenia in Tauris*, the necessary presence of the chorus forces Euripides into a gross absurdity, which is to form a secret plot in their hearing. (III, 317–18)[16]

Drama as we now know it, Kames declares, does not usually involve a chorus; consequently, the critic has no logical reason for insisting that the unities of time and place be preserved. In an amusing note, Kames scores Bossu for insisting on them: "Bossu, after observing, with wonderful critical sagacity, that winter is an improper season for an epic poem, and night not less improper for tragedy; admits however, that an epic poem may be spread through the whole summer months, and a tragedy through the whole sun-shine hours of the longest summer-day. . . . At this rate an English tragedy may be longer than a French tragedy; and in Nova Zembla the time of a tragedy and of an epic poem may be the same" (III, 300n.).

In short, Kames concludes, it is no more difficult for the mind to shift from place to place or from time to time in drama than it is for the mind to make the initial suspension of disbelief which drama demands and to convince the observer that he is in London during some previous historical period. A man can make these shifts when he looks at a series of historical paintings; it should be no more difficult for him to do it while watching a play: "And indeed, it must appear ridiculous, that a critic, who makes no difficulty of supposing candlelight to be sun-shine, or some painted canvasses a palace or a prison, should affect so much difficulty in imagining a latitude of place or of time in the story, beyond what is necessary in the representation" (III, 306).

VI *The Natural Garden*

Although it may surprise some readers to find a discussion of gardening in a book devoted to the theory of criticism, gardening has traditionally been considered one of the fine arts along with poetry, painting, and music. A theory of naturalism in the arts would therefore logically include some observations about

[113]

the qualities of an esthetically pleasing garden, and Kames presents his views in Chapter XXIV.

Beginning with the premise that gardening "... is not an inventive art, but an imitation of nature" (III, 341), Kames argues that the so-called formal garden, which had recently had its most extreme expression at Versailles, was essentially unnatural. Every reader, I am sure, has seen photographs of these gardens with their many fountains; their long, broad avenues, radiating out on four sides of the palace; and their flowers, trees, and hedges arranged in geometric shapes. For Kames such a garden was "stiff and artificial," a poor imitation of nature. He objected most strongly to such perversions of nature at Versailles as statues of beasts spouting water and trees cut into the shape of animals:

As gardening is not an inventive art, but an imitation of nature, or rather nature itself ornamented; it follows necessarily, that every thing unnatural ought to be rejected with disdain. Statues of wild beasts vomiting water, a common ornament in gardens, prevails in those of Versailles.... A lifeless statue of an animal pouring out water, may be endured without much disgust: but here the lions and wolves are put in violent action; each has seized its prey, a deer or a lamb, in act to devour: and yet, instead of extended claws and open mouth, the whole, as by a hocus-pocus trick, is converted into a different scene: the lion, forgetting his prey, pours out water plentifully; and the deer, forgetting its danger, performs the same operation; a representation not less absurd than that in the opera, where Alexander the Great, after mounting the wall of a town besieged, turns about and entertains his army with a song.... I have often amused myself with a fanciful resemblance betwixt these gardens and the Arabian tales. Each of them is a performance intended for the amusement of a great king: in the sixteen gardens of Versailles there is no unity of design, more than in the thousand and one Arabian tales: and, lastly, they are equally unnatural; groves of *jets d'eau*, statues of animals conversing in the manner of AEsop, water issuing out of the mouths of wild beasts, give an impression of fairy-land and witchcraft, not less than diamond-palaces, invisible rings, spells and incantations. (III, 341–45)

In contrast to such unnatural inventiveness, Kames defends two kinds of garden design which were quite fashionable in mid-century England, the so-called Paradise garden and the Chinese garden. Not to be confused with the tangled wilderness popular toward the end of the century, the Paradise garden sought to capture the feeling of nature before the fall, when it was full of variety and abundance, yet carefully tended by man. Kames quotes Milton's description of such a garden in *Paradise Lost:*

> Flowers worthy of paradise, which not nice art
> In beds and curious knots; but Nature boon
> Pour'd forth profuse on hill, and dale, and plain;
> Both where the morning-sun first warmly smote
> The open field, and where the unpierc'd shade
> Imbrown'd the noontide bow'rs. BOOK 4 (III, 339)

Such a garden could arouse in the spectator all emotions proper to a garden and do so in an orderly fashion. It could also take advantage of the intense emotional effect produced by contrast.

For the execution of such a natural garden, Kames suggests the advantage of winding walks rather than straight ones, the value of Gothic ruins, and at least one way to overcome the unpleasant artificiality of the star arrangement for the display of various plants: "This may be done by openings in the wood at various distances, which, in walking, bring successively under the eye every object as by accident: some openings display single objects, some a plurality in a line, and some a rapid succession of them. In this form, the mind at intervals is roused and cheared by agreeable objects; and the scene is greatly heightened by the surprise it occasions when we stumble, as it were, upon objects of which we had no expectation" (III, 340).

The Chinese garden, like the Paradise garden, never deviates from nature:

Nature is strictly imitated in the banks of their artificial lakes and rivers; which sometimes are bare and gravelly, sometimes covered with wood quite to the brink of the water. To flat spots adorned with flowers and shrubs, are opposed others steep and rocky. We see meadows covered with cattle; rice-grounds that run into lakes; groves into which enter navigable creeks and rivulets: these generally conduct to some interesting object, a magnificent building, terraces cut in a mountain, a cascade, a grotto, an artificial rock, and other such inventions. Their artificial rivers are generally serpentine; sometimes narrow, noisy, and rapid; sometimes deep, broad, and slow; and to make the scene still more active, mills and other moving machines are often erected. In the lakes are interspersed islands; some barren, surrounded with rocks and shoals; others inriched with every thing that art and nature can furnish. (III, 350–51)

Such a garden makes much more effective use of sudden contrast than does the Paradise garden, and Kames thoroughly approves of this usage: "The eye is conducted, from limited to extensive views, and from lakes and rivers to plains, hills, and woods: to dark and gloomy colours, are opposed the more brilliant: the different masses of light and shade are disposed in such a manner, as to render the composition distinct in its parts, and striking on the whole" (III, 352). Surprise and wonder are produced by streams which suddenly plunge underground or by dark caverns which suddenly terminate in a lush landscape.

Kames concludes his remarks about the esthetics of gardening with a plea for more attention to beauty of landscape on the college campus—an appeal which has a strangely modern ring. "It is a sad truth," he observes, "that the dirtiness and disorder of many colleges, . . . seldom fail to bring down the mind" (III, 355). Good professors, he goes on, perhaps contribute no more to a student's education than does the environment in which he lives. Oxford, the most distinguished of British universities, can take as much pride in its gardens as it does in its faculty.

VII *The Standard of Taste*

The final chapter of the book describes the ideal of sensibility with terms in which all the elements of criticism become meaningful. Kames reasserts what he has declared at the beginning of the book: the function of criticism is to nurture the man of taste. In Chapter XXV, Kames considers the proverb "There must be no disputing about taste." Following Hume's lead,[17] Kames points out that to accept this proposition is to accept complete relativism about the operation of the senses: "At this rate, a man is not within the reach of censure, even where, insensible to beauty, grandeur, or elegance, he prefers the Saracen's head upon a sign-post before the best tablature of Raphael, or a rude Gothic tower before the finest Grecian building: or where he prefers the smell of a rotten carcass before that of the most odoriferous flower: or jarring discords before the most exquisite harmony" (III, 401–2).

But common sense tells us that human nature is uniform among all men, as Kames has maintained regularly throughout *Elements;* and he asserts once again that: "We have a sense or conviction of a common nature, ... and our conviction is verified by experience. ... This common nature is conceived to be a model or standard for each individual that belongs to the kind" (III, 406). Since all men have a common nature, it is reasonable to conclude that the standard of taste represents an ideal possible for all men. Kames believes that man is capable of learning refinement and discrimination in the fine arts. The principles set forth in *Elements,* Kames declares, can help man to achieve such a sensibility.

András Horn, whose recent article is the best discussion of Kames's esthetic theory yet to appear, argues that Kames finally puts beauty in the same critical perspective as he does taste. Thus, beauty is essentially a secondary, not a primary, quality that exists "in the eye of the beholder" rather than in an object. And yet, Kames insists, beauty has an objective value because of the common nature of man. On the other hand, it is obvious that all men do not have the same idea about beauty. Horn calls this position "factual relativity."[18] Kames's conclusion is that all men have the potential to respond in the same way to beauty even though at any given historical moment only a "decisive minority" so respond.[19] Horn summarizes this insight succinctly: "Thus the concept of the 'decisive minority' implies that a work of art may represent an objective, though only potential value in spite of the factual relativity of the aesthetic judgments relating to it."[20]

The idea of development in man figures even more strongly in Kames's next book, *Sketches of the History of Man,* where he considers both man's abstract possibilities for growth and the real progress he has made during the course of human history. In *Elements* Kames stresses that "delicacy of taste," an ideal possible for all men, is in fact restricted to the rather rare combination of qualities which accompany civilization and culture: "... men, originally savage and brutal, acquire not rationality nor any delicacy of taste, till they be long disciplined in society. . . . Those who depend for food on bodily labour, are totally void of taste; of such a taste at least as can be of use in the fine arts. This consideration bars the greater part of mankind; and of the remaining part, many have their taste corrupted to such a degree as to unqualify them altogether for voting. The common sense of mankind must then be confined to the few that fall not under these exceptions" (III, 417–20). In *Sketches,* as we shall see in the next chapter, Kames reveals some unusually interesting ways in which the development of the human species has occurred.

CHAPTER 5

Sketches of the History of Man:
Human Origin and Development

SKETCHES, which appeared in 1774, represents Lord Kames's contribution to the developing science of natural history. In a way, the book is a compendium of Kames's thought; indeed, he refers to it in one place as his *magnum opus. Sketches* was addressed to an audience quite different from that to which *Essays* and *Elements* would appeal, an audience Kames quite frankly describes as middle class. "It is not intended for the learned; they are above it: nor for the vulgar; they are below it. It is intended for men, who, equally removed from the corruption of opulence, and from the depression of bodily labour, are bent on useful knowledge; who, even in the delirium of youth, feel the dawn of patriotism, and who in riper years enjoy its meridian warmth."[1]

As J. B. Black has indicated, Kames took little risk in writing natural history for a popular audience; a taste for history was the most distinguishing quality of the reading public in the later eighteenth century. "In all probability there has never been a period when history was so much in demand among the reading public in all European countries as in the latter part of the eighteenth century. It would be no exaggeration to say that the vogue of historical books between 1750 and the outbreak of the French Revolution was as great as the vogue of poetical literature in the age of Shakespeare and of the novel in the age of Scott."[2]

Kames regarded *Sketches* as a means of popularizing theories and beliefs which he had put forward in such earlier works as *Essays* and *Elements.* Thus one finds discussions of the nature of the mind, the discrimination of internal senses, intuition, and morality. It is in *Sketches* that Kames modifies his earlier theory,

developed in *Essays,* that determinism rather than free will motivates human action. In addition to reworking these familiar ideas,
he develops several interesting theories which had not been fully
worked out in his earlier writings. These final two chapters are
devoted to a discussion of two such concepts: first, his theory of
natural history, particularly in terms of the origin and development of the human race; second, his theory about the authenticity
and esthetic merit of the poems of Ossian. Kames was a firm believer in the authenticity of these poems which Macpherson had
"discovered," and his discussion of them offers some important
insights into eighteenth-century sensibility.

I *Primitivism and Progress*

In *Sketches* Lord Kames addresses himself to two of the most
important topics in the second half of the eighteenth century,
primitivism and progress. Sometimes regarded as completely op-
posing views of the origin and development of man, sometimes
considered to be equally valuable ways of describing human history, the debate over primitivism and progress continued in a
more anthropological and less cultural way the old controversy
between the ancients and the moderns.[3] In its most popular
form, the quarrel centered on the relative value of Classical
versus modern literature. Swift immortalized the literary war between his friend Temple and the scholar Richard Bentley over
the writings of Phalaris in *The Battle of the Books.*

But the ancient/modern controversy extended far beyond literary questions to include all human preoccupations. And writers did not all necessarily side with either ancients or moderns.
Some, like Louis Leroy in the sixteenth century (*De la viscissi-
tude ou variété des choses en l'univers*) proposed a cyclical theory of history, according to which a golden age may have already
occurred but would also occur again. The debate over primitivism and progress had a similar diversity. Those on the side of
primitivism and against progress could argue that human history
has been the record of degeneration from an ideal state of nature. Such an unequivocal position was rare, for the other side of
the coin was more common—the Hobbesian view that man in the
state of nature was a savage brute and that his history has been
a record of progress. Most writers, however, preferred a modi-

[120]

fied cyclical theory which could include both elements of primitivism and progress. Man had enjoyed a golden age after emerging from his original state of nature; society and luxury had combined to cause his degeneration; but there remained the possibility that he would overcome these forces to achieve again a state of perfection. Lord Kames comes closest to the third position, but his Calvinist environment makes him rather unwilling to predict the ultimate reformation of man.

II *Monboddo, Rousseau, and Kames*

A. O. Lovejoy, in an important essay on natural history, "Monboddo and Rousseau" makes with characteristic lucidity several discriminations about primitivism and progress. This essay is especially important for the student interested in Kames because Lovejoy takes for his subject another notable Scottish man of letters, James Burnet, Lord Monboddo. Monboddo, a colleague of Lord Kames on the judiciary bench, published in 1773 the first volume of his major work, *Of the Origin and Progress of Language.* Ian Ross has argued that Kames wrote *Sketches,* in part at least, as a rejoinder to Monboddo's book,[4] and thus a general knowledge of the ideas in *Origin* helps us understand Kames's positions in *Sketches.* Actually, the similarities between Kames and Monboddo are as striking as the differences between them. Both attempted to establish some sort of viable compromise between primitivism and progress, and both ultimately involved themselves in inconsistencies.[5] Lovejoy's essay links Monboddo and the French naturalist, Jean-Jacques Rousseau. Thus, Kames's theories can be conveniently related to both of these important eighteenth-century writers.

First, Lovejoy points out that, for Monboddo and Rousseau, man's original condition, the so-called state of nature, was "a condition of pure animality, in which our ancestors possessed no language, no social organization, almost no practical arts, and in general were in no way distinguished from the apes in intellectual attainments or modes of life." Second, it follows, that the state of nature "was not an ideal state, except with regard to the physical condition of the human animal." Lovejoy's third point is that, for Monboddo, the orangutang and man are of the same species; "in other words, that the orang-outangs are a portion of the human race who, for some reason, have failed to develop as the rest of it has done." Kames, as we shall see, equivocated about the original condition of man, viewing it at one point as savage and brutal; at another, as ideal. He would not agree with Monboddo, however, that man was ever indistinguishable from the apes.

Kames's ideas are much closer to Monboddo and Rousseau with regard to Lovejoy's fourth, fifth, and sixth points. Fourth, man has a potential for development which the rest of nature lacks. He may not have always exercised this *perfectibilité*, as Rousseau called it, but he has always had "a capacity for the gradual unfolding of higher intellectual faculties." Fifth, therefore, "human history—at least up to a certain point—should be regarded, not as it had very commonly been regarded, as a process of decline from a primitive perfection, a gradual dimming of the pure light of nature by which men had at first been illumined, but rather as a slow painful ascent from animality, through savagery, to the life of a rational and social being." Finally, a "new historical science" was needed which would acknowledge this pattern of development in man and make a searching study of contemporary man, especially as he exists in savage tribes, to document his continuing development through "the successive stages of this process of intellectual development and social evolution."[6]

III *The Races of Man*

Kames's view of the original state of nature differs from that of Monboddo and Rousseau; for, in the first essay of *Sketches,* "Diversity of Men and of Languages," he asserts that man is and has always been distinct from animals. All nature is stable; no "organic evolution"[7] occurs in any creature. Kames's proof for this is his customary one, common-sense: ". . . we have an innate sense, that each kind is endued with properties peculiar to itself; and that these properties belong to every individual of the kind . . . neither experience nor argument is required to prove, that a horse is not an ass, or that a monkey is not a man" (*Sketches,* I, 2–3). Kames rejects the more scientific arguments of Buffon and Linnaeus that the genus and species of creatures can be determined by their copulative practices or by the size and shape of their teeth.

We must not conclude from the foregoing, however, that man is a single race. The fact is, Kames declares, that man is divided into several races, each substantially different from the others. Here we find his antievolutionism in its purest form. Buffon, Montesquieu, and others had argued that creatures could adapt to their surroundings and that what appear to be several races of man are simply the result of man's adaptation to climate. Man remains substantially the same, only accidentally different. The two French naturalists had emphasized different aspects of the adaptation argument. Buffon had argued that physical changes occur in men because of climate; Montesquieu had stressed the effect of climate on human psychology.

Kames objects to both theories: "... is [Buffon] seriously of opinion, that any operation of climate or of other accidental cause, can account for the copper colour and smooth chin universal among the Americans, the prominence of the *pudenda* among the Hottentot women, or the black nipple no less universal among female Samoides? ... It is in vain to ascribe to the climate the low stature of the Esquimaux, the smallness of their feet, or the overgrown size of their head" (I, 12). In America, where there is a variety of climates, Kames continues, all the natives are copper-skinned. And generations of races have been transplanted from their original climates without any change in their complexion (I, 13–14). Kames appears to have no sense of anthropological time. If a black man brought to England does not change color overnight, the argument about the effect of climate is refuted!

Montesquieu proposed that climate affects the disposition of men, that in hot climates "people are timid like old men" and that in cold climates "bold like young men." To maintain this, Kames declares, "is to maintain, that the torrid zone is an unfit habitation for men; that they degenerate in it, lose their natural vigour, and even in youth become like old men" (I, 31). On the contrary, says Kames, observation proves that there is no relation between climate and courage; indeed, the very opposite of what Montesquieu claimed may be true. Thus the Laplanders, living in a cold climate, are notably pusillanimous; and Malayans are courageous although they live in a hot climate.

The fact is that there are many races of men, each with different physical and psychological qualities, each with a different language. And this variety is blessed by Providence: " 'God created many pairs of the human race, differing from each other both externally and internally; . . . he fitted these pairs for different climates, and placed each pair in its proper climate; . . . the peculiarities of the original pairs were preserved entire in their descendents; who, having no assistance but their natural talents, were left to gather knowledge from experience, and in particular were left (each tribe) to form a language for itself' " (I, 38–39).

Scripture poses something of a problem for this historical hypothesis. According to Genesis, God created the human race from a single pair in the beginning, and they existed in a state of innocence. Kames's solution to this problem is ingenious. There are really two creation stories in the Bible, he says; the one concerns Adam and Eve; the other, the incident of the Tower of Babel. In the second account, God punished disobedient and presumptuous man by bringing about a terrible convulsion which confused his language and scattered him all over the earth. Man lost his innocence and became savage. In effect, Kames concludes, God had changed the human race into human races: ". . . to harden them for their new habitations, it was necessary that they should be divided into different kinds, fitted for different climates" (I, 40).[8]

IV   *The Cycle of Human History*

Kames equivocates on the second of Lovejoy's discriminations about natural history—that the state of nature was not an ideal state, but was savage and brutal. In the earlier work, *Essays on Principles of Morality and Natural Religion* (1751), his ideas fit Lovejoy's description perfectly: "If we can trust history, the original inhabitants of this earth were a brutish and a savage race. And we have little reason to doubt of this fact, when, even at this day, we find the same sort of people in distant corners, who have no communication with the rest of mankind. The state of nature is accordingly represented by all writers, as a state of war; nothing going on but rapine and bloodshed."[9]

By 1774, however, Kames is not quite so committed to this point of view. He speculates about a pre-Babel state of innocence, as we have seen above; but he is not consistent about it.

Even in the natural order, however, he maintains that there are indications of an original state of innocence: "In the earliest stages of society . . . when the earth was still thinly populated and there was no contest over food and land, men lived innocently and cordially together: they had no irregular appetites, nor any ground of strife. In that state, moral principles joined their influence with that of national affection, to secure individuals from harm. Savages accordingly, who have plenty of food, and are simple in habitation and cloathing, seldom trasgress [*sic*] the rules of morality within their own tribe."[10] Or again, "In a nascent society, where men hunt and fish in common, where there is plenty of game, and where the sense of property is faint, mutual affection prevails, because there is no cause of discord" (I, 379). Such a view of the state of nature would, of course, accord with Kames's theory that man has an innate moral sense. The Caledonian civilization which the poet Ossian describes was quite likely living in this original state of benevolence.

But man did not remain long in such a state. Through some traumatic disordering, such as Babel, or through closer proximity with his neighbors as population increased, man degenerated to the savage state in which he may still be found in some aboriginal tribes. The cycle of human history does not, of course, stop with this degeneration; for, out of primitivism, comes progress. In the long ages between this savage state and the eighteenth century, man developed remarkably in his awareness of himself and his environment. The remaining essays in *Sketches* record this progress. Many have the term "progress" in their titles: progress in food and population; progress in understanding of property; progress in commerce, in the arts, in manners, in government, in reason, in morality, and in theology.

Progress does not bring blessedness to man. Most eighteenth-century primitivists realized that, carried far enough, progress leads to luxury, luxury to degeneration, and the whole cycle must begin again. "In all times," writes Kames, "luxury has been the ruin of every state where it prevailed. Nations are originally poor and virtuous. They advance to industry, commerce, and perhaps to conquest and empire. But this state is never permanent: great opulence opens a wide door to indolence, sensuality, corruption, prostitution, perdition."[11]

V *Progress in the Fine Arts*

The more advanced man becomes, the more leisure he has to be creative. "Arts accordingly make the quickest progress in a fertile soil, which produces plenty with little labour. Arts flourished early in Egypt and Chaldea, countries extremely fertile" (I, 88). Development of the arts is also related to prosperity and peace. The arts flourished in Athens and again in Rome during the reign of Augustus. "The restoration of the royal family in England, which put an end to a cruel and envenomed civil war, promoted improvements of every kind" (I, 102).

Kames's theory of progress lends support to his idea that taste in the fine arts is acquired with difficulty and remains the possession of a very few. In terms of human history, Kames declares, good taste is a new phenomenon. Man in his early stages of development lacked sensibility. Imagination was allowed to roam unchecked. "Wonder is the passion of savages and of rustics; to raise which, nothing is necessary but to invent giants and magicians, fairy-land and inchantment" (I, 107). Progress beyond this romantic taste was slow. And even when more mature literary forms took the place of romance, the language often remained immature: "When gigantic fictions were banished, some remaining taste for the wonderful encouraged gigantic similes, metaphors, and allegories" (I, 107). Kames gives a marvelous example of this "puerile" use of figurative language in the sermon of a bishop at the opening of the Council of Trent, and what most rankles Kames is the imprecise use of analogy:

He proves, that a council is necessary; because several councils have extirpated heresy, and deposed kings and emperors; because the poets assemble councils of the gods; because Moses writes, that at the creation of man and at confounding the language of the giants, God acted in the manner of a council; because religion has three heads, doctrine, sacraments, and charity, and that these three are termed *a council*. He exhorts the members of the council to strict unity, like the heroes in the Trojan horse. He asserts, that the gates of paradise and of the council are the same; that the holy fathers should sprinkle their dry hearts with the living water that flowed from it; and that otherwise the Holy Ghost would open their mouths like those of Balaam and Caiphas. (I, 110)

Kames criticizes the medieval mystery plays for their "gross manners," (I, 111) and medieval moralities for introducing "supernatural and allegorical beings upon the same stage with men and women" (I, 112). Renaissance comedy also lacks taste, for "to draw amusement from folly, real or pretended, is below the dignity of human nature" (I, 112). But censure is not reserved for older literature. Dryden is criticized for the "coarse stuff" and "out of place" scenes in his plays. French Enlightenment drama, "celebrated for refinement of taste," errs by "introducing Heathen Deities as actors in a real history" (I, 115).

Such unnatural practices can only be improved when sentiment takes the place of romance and when more mature feeling succeeds wonder. Kames is pleased that the "absurd romances that delighted the world for ages ... are now fallen into contempt every where. Madame de la Fayette led the way to novels in the present mode. She was the first who introduced sentiments instead of wonderful adventures, and amiable men instead of bloody heroes. In substituting distresses to prodigies, she made a discovery that persons of taste and feeling are more attached by compassion than by wonder" (I, 107).

Classical literature must be submitted to the same test of taste. In the quotation below, Kames criticizes the Homeric epics for their lack of refinement; and Greek drama fares no better. The very vastness of the Greek theater made the communication of refined feeling impossible:

No human voice could fill the Greek theatre, which was so spacious as to contain several thousands without crowding. A brass pipe was invented to strengthen the voice; but that invention suppressed the melody of pronunciation, by confining the voice to a harsh monotony. The pipe was not the only unpleasant circumstance; every actor wore a mask; for what end or purpose, is not explained. It may be true, that the expressions of the countenance could not be distinctly seen by those who occupied the back rows; and a mask possibly was thought necessary in order to put all the citizens upon a level. But without prying into the cause, let us only figure an actor with a mask and a pipe. He may represent tolerably a simple incident or plain thought, such as are the materials of an Italian opera; but the voice, countenance, and gestures, are indispensable in expressing refined sentiments, and the more delicate tones of a passion. (I, 140–41)

In a remarkable judgment which indicates how little Kames understood the intellectual and religious turmoil that produced Greek tragedy, he states "that it was not the dialogue which chiefly enchanted the Athenians, nor variety in the passions represented, nor perfection in the actors, but machinery and pompous decoration, joined with exquisite music" (I, 141).

Greek and Roman comedy impressed Kames no more than Greek tragedy. Greek comedy, he writes, went through various stages from Aristophanes to Menander. The comedies of Aristophanes "err not less against taste than against decency" by representing real persons on the stage (I, 144). Menander improved things very little, judging by the plays of his imitator, Plautus, who "shows very little art, either in his compositions, or in the conduct of his pieces" (I, 144). Kames objects to the simplemindedness of Plautus's plots and to the unnaturalness of having soliloquies delivered in a public street. "His wit consists almost entirely in a play of words, an eternal jingle, words brought together that have nearly the same sound, with different meanings, and words of different sounds that have the same meaning... Plautus is full of tautologies, and digressions very little to the purpose" (I, 145). The other Roman comic dramatist, Terence, fares somewhat better. Kames notes his superior skills in plotting and the greater naturalness of his style, which is free from the "bastard wit" of Plautus. "The dialogue... of Terence is more natural and correct, not a word but to the purpose" (I, 145). Both Roman playwrights limit themselves to a few characters, and these are types. He attributes this lack of naturalism to a "defect of knowledge."

Once again, human history does not move in a straight line. True taste or refinement in the arts never lasts long. "An art, in its progress toward maturity, is greatly promoted by emulation; and after arriving at maturity, its downfall is not less promoted by it. It is difficult to judge of perfection but by comparison; and an artist, ambitious to outstrip his predecessors, cannot submit to be an imitator, but must strike out something new, which in an art advanced to ripeness, seldom fails to be a degeneracy" (I, 150–51). Vocal music, for example, had been developed by the Greeks into a perfect blend of thought and feeling. The forte of Greek music was melody uncluttered by harmony. "Artists in later times, ignorant why harmony was so little regarded by the ancients, apply'd themselves seriously to its cultivation; and they have been wonderfully successful. But they have been successful at the expense of melody; which in modern compositions, generally speaking, is lost amid the blaze of harmony" (I, 151). Loyal Scots like Kames especially resented the increasing popularity of Italian music in Scotland. Italian music was, of course, richly harmonious; but "These compositions," says Kames, "tickle the ear by the luxury of complicated sounds, but make seldom any impression on the heart" (I, 151).

CHAPTER 6

Sketches of the History of Man:
Anthropology and Criticism

IN the years between 1760 and 1763 James Macpherson published his translation of ancient Celtic poetry and began what
was to prove the most controversial and traumatic episode in
the history of eighteenth-century Scottish literature. Sponsored
at first by the Edinburgh literati, Macpherson's translations
purported to be English versions of bardic poems ranging from
short lyrics to two epics which had been composed in the third
century by a Caledonian poet named Ossian. A great debate
ensued almost immediately over the authenticity of the poems.
It involved many notable literary figures of the day including, in
England, Johnson, Gray, Horace Walpole, and Burke; and in
Scotland, David Hume, John Home the dramatist, Robertson,
Blair, and Kames. Macpherson added fuel to the fire by
haughtily refusing to produce the manuscripts from which the
translations had been made. Some patriotic Scots have continued to fight the battle for the last two hundred years. An
Edinburgh edition of the poems published in this century notes
in its introduction that "the rumour of the Ossianic controversy has not yet died away."[1] More germane to the issue than
patriotism, however, were the various ideas about primitivism
then in vogue (which were discussed earlier in Chapter 5) and a
relatively new kind of critical theory, ultimately to be labeled
"historicism," which was replacing the formal categories of neo-
Classicism.

I   The Ossianic Controversy

Before considering Lord Kames's contribution to the controversy, we should briefly review its major incidents.[2]   In 1759

John Home met Macpherson in Dumfriesshire where the latter was tutoring. In the course of their conversation Macpherson told Home of his love of ancient Celtic poetry and of his habit of translating fragments of the poems from time to time. Home, struck by the beauty of the translations, encouraged Macpherson to publish them. *Fragments of Ancient Poetry* appeared in 1760 with an introduction by Hugh Blair.

The Edinburgh literati were excited at the propect of recovering their lost literary heritage; and several, David Hume and Robertson among them, agreed to finance a trip to the Highlands for Macpherson to collect "larger and more complete pieces of poetry which he informed them he knew to exist there, and of which some of the fragments already published were small detached parts. He particularly mentioned a poem of an epic form, of considerable length on the subject of the wars of the renowned Fion, or Fingal, (a name familiar to every ear in the remote parts of the Highlands), which he thought might be collected entire."[3] Macpherson was as good as his word. In 1762 he published *Fingal,* an epic poem in six books, along with several shorter heroic poems. This was followed in 1763 by the publication of his translation of another Caledonian epic, *Temora,* in eight books. Macpherson included the original Gaelic of one of the books of *Temora* and promised to get the others into print as soon as it was convenient. He never fulfilled his promise.

The ripples of skepticism which had greeted the publication of *Fragments* became a tide after the appearance of *Fingal.* Gray had written in 1760: "Very few admire [the poems], and almost all take them for fiction."[4] Horace Walpole read the manuscript of *Fingal* at Macpherson's invitation and commented several months before its publication in a letter to George Montagu: *"Fingal* is come out ... I will trust with a secret, but you must not disclose it; I should be ruined by my Scottish friends; in short, I cannot believe it genuine."[5] In London in 1763 David Hume heard nothing but disbelief in the poems; to the coffee-house set, the poems were "a palpable and impudent forgery."[6]

Hume, who was becoming more and more convinced that the Edinburgh literati had been duped, wrote in September, 1763, to one of Macpherson's most stalwart backers, Hugh Blair, whose appreciation and defense of the poems, *A Critical Dissertation on the Poems of Ossian, Son of Fingal,* had just appeared.[7] In his letter, Hume urged Blair to get more credible evidence of the poems' authenticity:

I live in a place where I have the pleasure of frequently hearing justice done to your Dissertation, but never heard it mentioned in a company, where some one person or other did not express his doubts with regard to the authenticity of the Poems which are its subject, and I often hear them totally rejected, with disdain and indignation, as a palpable and most impudent forgery. This opinion has indeed become very prevalent among the men of letters in London; and I can foresee, that in a few years, the poems, if they continue to stand on their present footing, will be thrown aside, and will fall into final oblivion... there are... internal reasons against them, particularly from the manners, notwithstanding all the art with which you have endeavoured to throw a varnish on that circumstance; and the preservation of such long and such connected poems, by oral tradition alone, during a course of fourteen centuries, is so much out of the ordinary course of human affairs, that it requires the strongest reason to make us believe it.... I was told by Burke, a very ingenious Irish gentleman, the author of a tract on the Sublime and Beautiful, that on the first publication of Macpherson's book, all the Irish cried out, *We know all those poems; we have always heard them from our infancy;* but when he asked more particular questions, he could never learn that any one had ever heard or could repeat the original of any one paragraph of the pretended translation.[8]

Blair never manged to get convincing evidence. By 1773 Macpherson was generally regarded as a forger south of the Scottish border. In that year Samuel Johnson traveled to the Hebrides and returned convinced more than ever that Macpherson knew little Gaelic and had perpetrated a hoax. With characteristic vigor Johnson announced this fact to his London admirers and this so enraged Macpherson that he challenged the sixty-six-year-old Johnson to a duel. Johnson's letter in reply rivals his famous letter to Lord Chesterfield, written nearly twenty years before.[9] His remarks on Homer refer to a translation of the *Iliad* which Macpherson had just recently completed:

MR. JAMES McPHERSON—I received your foolish and impudent note. Whatever insult is offered me I will do my best to repel, and what I cannot do for myself the law will do for me. I will not desist from detecting what I think a cheat from any fear of the menaces of a Ruffian.

You want me to retract. What shall I retract? I thought your book an imposture from the beginning. I think it upon yet surer reasons an imposture still. For this opinion I give the publick my reasons which I here dare you to refute.

But however I may despise you, I reverence truth and if you can prove the genuineness of the work I will confess it. Your rage I defy, your abilities since your Homer, are not so formidable, and what I have heard of your morals disposes me to pay regard not to what you shall say, but to what you can prove.

You may print this if you will.

SAM. JOHNSON[10]

With such prestigious writers as David Hume and Johnson questioning the authenticity of the translations, how could Lord Kames, who most certainly had followed the debate, have possibly defended them and have done so as late as 1774. The answer lies, first of all, in an understanding of just what Macpherson had done; and then in Kames's theory of primitivism and historicism. While Johnson, Hume, and others thought that Macpherson's work was a complete forgery, later investigation revealed that his translations were related at least in part to the oral tradition of Gaelic poetry which existed in the Highlands in the mid-eighteenth century. Many witnesses during the investigation of the Highland Committee testified to knowing of ballads and poems about Fingal and Ossian which sounded like the originals of Macpherson's translations.

All agreed, however, that his knowledge of Gaelic was questionable and that his translations were always open to charges of inaccuracy; but the judgment of the Committee was that it would be fairer to call Macpherson a fabricator than a forger. "[The Committee] is inclined to believe that he was in use to supply chasms, and to give connection, by inserting passages which he did not find, and to add what he conceived to be dignity and delicacy to the original composition, by striking out passages, by softening incidents, by refining the language, in short by changing what he considered as too simple or too rude for a modern ear, and elevating what in his opinion was below the standard of good poetry."[11] More recent scholarship has revealed that in *Fingal* Macpherson drew on twelve authentic Gaelic sources and that he was probably familiar with the most important written collection of Gaelic heroic poetry, *The Book of the Dean of Lismore.*[12]

II *Primitivism and Poetry*

Kames would, of course, have known about the oral tradition of Gaelic poetry; and this knowledge along with a certain patriotic pride, may have somewhat influenced his defense of the authenticity of the translations. More important, however, was his theory of primitivism discussed in Chapter 5. As was noted there, Kames had given up, possibly through the influence of Rousseau, his earlier Hobbesian view, expressed in *Essays on the Principles of Morality and Natural Religion,* that man was by nature selfish and that society served to protect man from himself. In *Sketches* he proposes that man in his original state was peaceful and benevolent, and that only through later social pressures, caused by increasing numbers, did he become savage. He then began to progress slowly toward civilization and, having achieved it, was in danger of repeating the cycle because of his propensity toward luxury. Donald Foerster has missed this cyclical ideal in Kames's thought in his otherwise excellent studies of Scottish criticism.[13] He sees a contradition in the fact that Kames praises the manners in Ossian, but criticizes those in Homer, even though Homer lived in a later and presumably "somewhat more refined period."[14] Actually, in terms of Kames's theory, we would expect the more primitive Ossian to reflect a less savage society than did Homer.

At any rate Kames saw in the Ossian poems a perfect illustration of his primitivistic theory. There was, of course, the matter of authenticity; but Kames saw no problem here. Proceeding on the assumption that a refined state, such as the poems describe, was possible for man in the earliest stage of his development—the so-called hunting stage—Kames develops two logical arguments for their authenticity. The fact that his conclusions were wrong does not detract from his inductive acuity, but testifies rather to Macpherson's abilities as a fabricator. His first argument rests on the assumption that the most persuasive description of a society will come from the poet who has actually lived in it: "It is a noted and well-founded observation, that manners are never painted to the life by anyone to whom they are not familiar" (*Sketches*, I, 282). The poems under question propose to describe man in his most primitive state. What convinces Kames that the poems are authentic is the fact that no reference to later stages of human development can be found in them. If the Ossian poems were fiction, as many were claiming, surely there would be some inconsistency, some incongruity in the manners described. But there is none:

Every scene in Ossian relates to hunting, to fighting, and to love, the sole occupations of men in the original state of society: there is not a single image, simile, nor allusion, but what is borrowed from that state, without a jarring circumstance. Supposing all to be mere invention, is it not amazing to find no mention of highland clans, nor of any name now in use? Is it not still more amazing, that there is not the slightest hint of the Christian religion, not even in a metaphor or allusion? Is it not equally amazing that in a work where deer's flesh is frequently mentioned, and a curious method of roasting it, there should be not a word of fish as food, which is so common in later times? Very few highlanders know that their forefathers did not eat fish; and supposing it to be known, it would require attention more than human, never once to mention it. Can it be supposed, that a modern writer could be so constantly on his guard, as never to mention corn, nor cattle? In a story so scanty of poetical images, the sedentary life of a shepherd, and the industry of a husbandman, would make a capital figure: the cloven foot would somewhere appear. And yet in all the works of Ossian, there is no mention of agriculture; and but a slight hint of a herd of cattle in one or two allusions. I willingly give all advantages to the unbeliever: Supposing the author of Ossian to be a late writer, embellished with every refinement of modern education; yet even upon that supposition he is a miracle, far from being equalled by any other author ancient or modern.[15]

In his second argument, Kames forgets the growing popularity of the "noble savage" idea, even though he accepts the idea himself. He states that no modern poet writing about a primitive age would have imagined its manners to be so refined as they are in Ossian. The paradox is so obvious and the danger of exposure so present that no writer would be foolish enough to do such a thing. This fact convinces Kames more than ever that the poems are indeed authentic: "... we are forced, however reluctantly, to believe, that these manners are not fictitious, but in reality the manners of his [Ossian's] country, coloured perhaps, or a little heightened, according to the privilege of an epic poet" (I, 284).

Kames supports his idea about the pattern of man's development by calling the reader's attention to several peoples other than the Caledonians who showed signs of the same benevolence in their early history. The Celtae in general "were upright in their dealings, and far removed from deceit and duplicity.... And tho' cruel to their enemies, yet Pomponius Mela observes, that they were kind and compassionate to the supplicant and unfortunate. Strabo describes the Gauls, as studious of war, and of great alacrity in fighting; otherwise an innocent people, altogether void of malignity" (I, 303–4). The Scandinavians show a similar refinement in their early history, and Kames points out several parallels between the manners described in the Edda literature and those described in the Ossian poems. An elevation of mind, a love of fame, a bardic tradition, an elevated tone in language, and a courtesy toward women are found in both cultures:

...if authentic history be relied on, we can entertain no doubt, that the manners of the Gallic and British Celtae, including the Caledonians, were such as are above described. And as the manners ascribed by Ossian to his countrymen the Caledonians, are in every particular conformable to those now mentioned, it clearly follows, that Ossian was no inventor, but drew his pictures of manners from real life. (I, 307)

In the Scandinavian manners ... is discovered a striking resemblance to those described by Ossian. And as such were the manners of the Scandinavians in the first stage of society, it no longer remains a wonder, that the manners of Caledonia should be equally pure in the same early period. And now every argument above urged in favour of Ossian as a genuine historian has its full weight, without the least counterpoise. (I, 326)

III *Historicism and Esthetics*

Kames is concerned not only with the authenticity of the Ossian poems but also with their literary merit. To understand his judgments, the reader must first be reminded of certain changes in critical values which occurred in the eighteenth century. In an article already referred to, Donald Foerster speaks of a shift in emphasis from the esthetic to the historical —from an interest in the work of art as art to an interest in the work as a reflection of the period in which it was composed.[16] His notion that the esthetic and the historical approaches are incompatible is misleading and must be viewed in relation to the more comprehensive discriminations made by R. S. Crane.[17] Crane supports Foerster's contention that the shift in critical values meant a rejection of neo-Classicism with its emphasis on the imitation of ideal generic models. He also recognizes the emergence of historical criticism during this period, but sees it in relation to a more important fact—an emphasis on audience rather than on models for the determination of artistic merit. What is natural is of increasing interest and it is defined as that which will please men of sensibility.

This emphasis on audience as esthetic norm goes even further. If the writer learns what will please by the study of human nature and if the best poetry is in effect that which represents the best human qualities, then the esthetic response becomes not a response to some distant ideal of art, but a response to that manifestation of human nature which the artist knows most perfectly, his own audience. The artist in effect tells his audience about itself. If the artist's society embodies the best in human nature, as did the society described in Ossian's poetry, then the re-creation of the society will be esthetically pleasing in an age when the best in human nature is once again understood. If the artist's society has degenerated from the state of innocence or has not progressed to a state of refined sensibility, then the poetry which such an artist produces can only reflect this degeneration. Thus Homer for all his genius is limited in his vision to his own historical environment, and there is much in his poetry which does not please. To return to Foerster's distinction once again, I should not say that the esthetic and the historical excluded each other, but rather that the esthetic response became more dependent on a knowledge of the artist's environment.

IV *Homer and Ossian*

The importance of historical factors for criticism can be seen most clearly in Kames's comparative study of Homer and Ossian. A refined sensibility, Kames states, is repelled by the historical realities in Homer and attracted to those in Ossian. Homer's age indulged in countless improprieties; Ossian presents a picture of social refinement and benevolence. What Kames objects to most vigorously in Homer is his particularity, "an endless number of minute circumstances, especially in the description of battles, where they are most improper. One capital beauty of an epic poem is the selection of such incidents and circumstances as to make a deep impression, keeping out of view everything low or familiar" (I, 149–50). Homer made no attempt to exclude the low and familiar, and his poems clearly illustrate Kames's charge that "No savages are more cruel than the Greeks and Trojans were" (I, 245). "Roughness and harshness of manners are generally connected with cruelty; and the manners of the Greeks and Trojans are accordingly represented . . . as remarkably rough and harsh" (I, 254).

Most of the illustrations Kames gives for this undignified particularity in Homer stand in clear contrast to the refinement of such manners in Ossian, as we shall see below "Homer's hero, tho' superior to all in bodily strength, takes every advantage of his enemy: and *never feels either compassion or remorse* [Italics mine]" (I, 265). Deceitfulness and willfulness are characteristic of both heroes and gods. "Homer paints his gods as mercenary to an extreme" (II, 409).

In Homer, even the great Jupiter makes no difficulty to send a lying dream to Agamemnon, chief of the Greeks. Dissimulation is recommended by the goddess Minerva. Ulysses declares his detestation at using freedom with truth: and yet no man deals more in feigned stories. In the 22nd book of the Iliad, Minerva is guilty of gross deceit and treachery to Hector. When he flies from Achilles, she appears to him in the shape of his brother Deiphobus, exhorts him to turn upon Achilles, and promises to assist him. Hector accordingly, returning to the fight, darts his lance; which rebounds from the shield of Achilles;

for by Vulcan it was made impenetrable. Hector calls upon his brother for another lance; but in vain, for Deiphobus was not there. The Greeks in Homer's time must have been strangely deformed in their morals, when such a story could be relished. (II, 326)

The crude manners of the Greeks extend to their eating habits and to their treatment of women. Kames notes that barbarians are not accustomed to regular meals and consequently can fast for long periods and then gorge themselves when a meal appears: "In the Iliad of Homer, book 9, Agamemnon calls a council at night in his tent. Before entering on business, they go to supper, (line 122). An embassy to Achilles is resolved on. The ambassadors again sup with Achilles on pork-griskins, (line 271). Achilles rejects Agamemnon's offer; and the same night Ulysses and Diomed set out on their expedition to the Trojan camp: returning before day, they had a third supper" (I, 331n.).

The heroes in the poem are frequently "crammed" with food. "The Greeks in their feasts distinguished their heroes by a double portion. Ulysses cut a fat piece out of the chine of a wild boar for Demodocus the bard ... Telemachus complains bitterly of Penelope's suitors, that they were gluttons and consumed his beef and mutton. The whole 14th book of the Odyssey, containing the reception of Ulysses by Eumaeus the swine-herd, is miserably low. Manners must be both gross and low, where common beggars are admitted to the feasts of princes, and receive scraps from their hands" (I, 262).

The Greeks in Homer also show none of that courtesy toward women which is everywhere apparent in Ossian:

Homer paints in lively colours the riches of the Phoeacians, their skill in navigation, the magnificence of the king's court, of his palace, and of the public buildings. But, with the same breath, he describes Nausicaa, the king's daughter, travelling to the river on a waggon of greasy cloaths, to be washed there by her and her maids. Possibly it will be urged, that such circumstances, however low in our opinion, might appear otherwise to the Greeks. If they had appeared low to the Greeks, they would not have been introduced by their greatest poet. But what does this prove, other than that the Greeks were low in their manners? Their manners did not correspond to the delicacy of their taste in the fine arts. Nor can it be expected that they should correspond, when the

Greeks were strangers to that polite society with woman which refines behaviour, and elevates manners. (I, 262–63)

Ossian's world is one of sentiment, a world as admirable and pleasurable to behold in the eighteenth century as it was in that ancient age. The heroes in the poem, unlike Homer's heroes, are humane, selfless, and benevolent: "...we find humanity blended with courage in all their actions" (I, 292). Kames describes their pursuit of fame, which he distinguishes from a similar pursuit in Homer: "In Homer's time, heroes were greedy of plunder, and, like robbers, were much disposed to insult a vanquished foe. According to Ossian, the ancient Caledonians had no idea of plunder: and as they fought for fame only, their humanity overflow'd to the vanquished" (I, 292). "Love of fame is painted by Ossian as the ruling passion of his countrymen the Caledonians. Warriors are everywhere described, as esteeming it their chief happiness to be recorded in the songs of the bards: that feature is never wanting in any of Ossian's heroes" (I, 285).

Kames's illustrations from Ossian reveal how difficult it may be for the modern reader to adopt the point of view of the age of sensibility. Many a modern reader, for example, would have difficulty finding the following passage morally edifying; but Kames and critics like him demanded this kind of moral communiqué from art: "Fingal speaks: 'Ullin, my aged bard, take the ship of the King. Carry Oscar to Selma, and let the daughters of Morven weep. We shall fight in Erin for the race of fallen Cormac. The days of my years begin to fail: I feel the weakness of my arm. My fathers bend from their clouds to receive their gray-hair'd son. But, Trenmor! before I go hence, one beam of my fame shall rise: in fame shall my days end, as my years begun: my life shall be one stream of light to other times' " (I, 286) .

Love of fame, kindness toward enemies, and heroic actions arise from a general pattern of feeling in the Ossian poems which Kames calls "elevated sentiments." Ossian's countrymen are even more remarkable for their "tender sentiments," and here the contrast with Homer is sharper. Kames quotes passage after passage to document such sentiments as parental affection, grief over the loss of children, and pathetic reflection on the brevity of life. He remarks on the fine touch which the poet

[140]

uses in the following passage, one which a certain kind of modern taste would once again find objectionable as art:

'We saw Oscar leaning on his shield: we saw his blood around. Silence darkened on the face of every hero: each turned his back and wept. The King strove to hide his tears. He bends his head over his son: and his words are mixed with sighs. And art thou fallen, Oscar, in the midst of thy course! The heart of the aged beats over thee. I see thy coming battles: I behold the battles that ought to come, but they are cut off from thy fame. When shall joy dwell at Selma? when shall the song of grief cease on Morven? My sons fall by degrees, Fingal will be the last of his race. The fame I have received will pass away: my age shall be without friends. I shall sit like a grey cloud in my hall: nor shall I expect the return of a son with his sounding arms. Weep, ye heroes of Morven; never more will Oscar rise.' (I, 290)

Ossian differs from Homer most notably in his treatment of women, which Kames maintains is a pattern of conduct most suggestive of the general manners of a nation (I, 296). While Homer treats women in a rather disrespectful fashion, Ossian held women in the highest regard. Such an attitude, Kames argues, must have been indigenous to the Caledonian culture. "Had the Caledonians made slaves of their women, and thought as meanly of them as savages commonly do, it could have never entered the imagination of Ossian, to ascribe to them those numberless graces that exalt the female sex, and render many of them objects of pure and elevated affection" (I, 301). Once again a series of illustrative passages follows and once again the passages are sentimental: "Her breasts were like foam on the wave, and her eyes like stars of light: her hair was dark as the raven's wing: her soul was generous and mild. My love for Moina was great: and my heart poured fourth in joy" (I, 298–99).

Modern taste may recoil against this kind of emotional expression. But perhaps the ability to write and respond to what this age called "sentiment" is not an ability which should be peremptorily dismissed as uncritically naïve. Indeed our own age, which has reversed the taste of the late eighteenth century and has almost entirely sublimated the natural expression of emotion, may have a good deal to learn from the much-maligned "man of feeling." He may provide some insights into how we may come to grips with our own neuroses.

CHAPTER 7

Conclusion

L ORD KAMES'S importance as a writer must ultimately be evaluated within the framework of eighteenth-century intellectual history. His major contribution to that history is a critical theory which, though derivative in part, represents the first comprehensive exposition of what might be called "empirical esthetics"—a critical theory which examines and modifies traditional judgments about beauty, taste, and form, and does so on the basis of actual experience. The most perceptive and original parts of his critical theory include the discussion of sympathy as esthetic norm, ideal presence, negative capability, and the heroic couplet. While he may have had a somewhat mechanistic notion of sympathy, he did nevertheless appreciate the intuitive element in man's esthetic experience. The major esthetic theorist writing immediately after Kames, Immanuel Kant, built his entire theory of beauty around a proper understanding of the intuitive experience. Kames's ideas about ideal beauty and negative capability anticipate, of course, the esthetic theories of Coleridge and Keats. Direct influence cannot be proven in either case, but *Elements of Criticism* was widely known in the schools; and Coleridge at least would also have learned of Kames's theories through the German critic Lessing. The discussion of the heroic couplet in *Elements* is without parallel, as far as I have been able to determine. Modern critics who feel that more attention should be given to the formal qualities of eighteenth-century versification could certainly profit from a study of Kames's analysis.

In eighteenth-century studies generally, it is becoming more and more fashionable to reject the "history of ideas" approach in flavor of some brand of new criticism, formalism, or structuralism. Essays proliferate which stress ingenuity at the expense of insight and understanding. Now I should not like to see us return to the extreme of reading the literature of the period solely for its intellectual content—I am not at all certain, I might add, that anyone ever adopted such a method; surely Lovejoy did not. But an appreciation of the ideas which Lord Kames treats in his three major works is essential to a proper reading of many eighteenth-century literary works. Fielding's moral vision can be looked at as a combination of sympathy and benevolence, ideas which grow out of the "moral sense" theory of human nature. Sterne is very much concerned with empirical psychology and with the principle of association. The central conflict in *Humphry Clinker* is between primitivism and progress. And both Johnson's *Rasselas* and Voltaire's *Candide* attack a simplistic theory of optimism, as does Kames himself in *Sketches of the History of Man.*

I think it can finally be said of Henry Home, Lord Kames, that he truly devoted himself to what Pope called "the proper study of mankind." For Kames had an unquenchable curiosity about man and about human society. He also had a passion for order, and each of his books concerns itself primarily with the discovery of order in human nature and in human institutions. In other works not discussed here, he proposes ways of discovering this order in law, in farming, and in education. Quite often we hear the Scottish Enlightenment criticized for the narrow-mindedness of its empirical approach, but the reader of this volume should appreciate the irony of such a judgment. Empiricism was never a method the Scots relied on exclusively. Not even the notorious infidel David Hume made such a fundamental error. For Lord Kames, wisdom was a challenging goal, not easily achieved. It demanded a total engagement of reason, intuition, and common sense. In his three major works Kames often manages to achieve this total engagement.

Notes and References

Chapter One

1. *Private Papers from Malahide Castle,* ed. Geoffrey Scott and Frederick Pottle, XV (Mount Vernon, New York, 1928–37), 260–316.

2. Helen W. Randall, "The Critical Theory of Lord Kames," *Smith College Studies in Languages and Literature,* XXII (1940–41), nos. 1–4.

3. Ian Ross, " 'The Most Arrogant Man in the World': The Life and Writings of Henry Home, Lord Kames," (Unpublished dissertation, University of Texas, 1960) p. 5.

4. Boswell, *op. cit.,* p. 268.

5. *Ibid.,* p. 269.

6. Ross, *op. cit.,* p. 9.

7. *Ibid.,* p. 11.

8. Quoted in Ross, p. 11.

9. Boswell, *op. cit.,* p. 271.

10. David Daiches, *The Paradox of Scottish Culture: The Eighteenth-Century Experience* (London, 1964), p. 7.

11. Ross, *op. cit.,* p. 134.

12. Henry Cockburn, *Memorials of His Time* (Edinburgh, 1856), pp. 117–18n. Quoted in Ross, p. 232.

13. Bodleian, Douce MS. 193, f.57 n/v. Quoted in Ross, pp. 233–35.

14. Ross, *op. cit.,* Chapter V.

15. *New Letters of David Hume,* ed. Raymond Klibansky and Ernest C. Mossner (Oxford, 1954), p. 1–2.

16. Randall, *op. cit.,* p. 12.

17. *Ibid.,* p. 9.

18. *Ibid.,* p. 15.

19. Ross, *op. cit.,* p. 154.

20. Randall, *op. cit.,* p. 18.

21. *Ibid.,* p. 19.

22. Randall, *ibid.,* pp. 77–81.

23. Miss Randall quotes substantial parts of the review on page 76. The translation is mine.

24. Boswell, *op. cit.,* pp. 300–02.

Chapter Two

1. *Essays in the History of Ideas* (New York, 1960), p. 79.

2. Leslie Stephen, *English Thought in the Eighteenth Century,* I (London, 1962), 20–21.

3. Thomas A. Hanzo, "Latitude and Restoration Criticism," *Anglistica,* XII (Copenhagen, 1961), 15.

4. Professor Hanzo makes this distinction and notes important treatments of the problem by Lovejoy and Watkins. See p. 46–52.

5. Stephen, *op. cit.,* p. 116. Roland N. Stromberg insists that a further distinction must be made between Deism and Christian rationalism. See "Lovejoy's 'Parallel' Reconsidered," *Eighteenth-Century Studies,* I (Summer, 1968), pp. 381–395.

6. Lovejoy, *op. cit.,* pp. 85–86.

7. Ross, *op. cit.,* p. 58.

8. *Essays on the Principles of Morality and Natural Religion* (Edinburgh, 1751) "Advertisement." All subsequent references are to this edition and are indicated in the text.

9. Basil Willey uses this phrase in *The Eighteenth-Century Background* (New York, 1941), p. 112.

10. Ross, *op. cit.,* p. 80.

11. Ed. L. A. Selby-Bigge (Oxford, 1888), p. 86.

12. *Ibid.,* p. 96.

13. Ross, *op. cit.,* pp. 94–95.

14. *The Scottish Philosophy, from Hutcheson to Balfour* (New York, 1875), pp. 2–6, 9.

Chapter Three

1. *William Blake* (New York, 1965), p. 1.

2. Helen W. Randall, *op. cit.,* p. 70.

3. Readers interested in this relationship between Kames and German esthetics should consult the following works: Josef Wohlgemuth, *Henry Homes Asthetik und ihr Einfluss auf deutsche Asthetiker* (Berlin, 1893); Wilhelm Neumann, *Die Bedeutung Home's fur die Asthetik und sein Einfluss auf die deutschen Asthetiker* (Halle, 1894); and Leroy R. Shaw, "Henry Home of Kames: Precursor of Herder," *Germanic Review,* XXXV (1960), 16–27.

4. *The Critical Review,* pp. 302–3. Quoted in Randall, p. 71.

5. Randall, p. v.

6. *Ibid.,* p. 23n.

7. See A. O. Lovejoy's essay on the various meanings of nature, "Nature as Aesthetic Norm," in *Essays in the History of Ideas,* pp. 69–77;

also Basil Willey, " 'Nature' in Literary Theory," *Eighteenth-Century Background*, pp. 18–26.

8. *Elements of Criticism,* 2nd edition, I (Edinburgh, 1763), p. 16. All subsequent references to *Elements* are to this three-volume edition and are indicated in the text.

9. See the discussion of the relation of associationism to art in Chapter IV, "The Growth of Individualism: The Premise of the Association of Ideas," in W. J. Bate's important study, *From Classic to Romantic* (Cambridge, 1946), pp. 93–128.

10. András Horn links Kame's ideas about association and art to the modern psychological principle of *Ganzheit,* according to which "man is constantly seeking out from among the impressions crowding upon his consciousness meaningful wholes or gestalts." See "Kames and the Anthropological Approach to Criticism," *Philological Quarterly,* XLIV (April, 1965), 214.

11. See W. J. Bate's excellent discussion of the relation of feeling to empirical psychology in Chapter V of *From Classic to Romantic,* "The Growth of Individualism: The Premise of Feeling," pp. 129–59.

12. Horn comments on the relation between "nature" and "sympathy" in the article referred to above. In the experience of sympathy, man recognizes that suffering is a part of his own nature. Kames works out the relation between the two in his treatment of tragedy in *Essays* in a section entitled "Of Our Attachment to Objects of Distress."

13. See Gordon McKenzie, "Lord Kames and the Mechanist Tradition," *Essays and Studies,* University of California Publications in English, XIV (1943), 93–121.

14. Kames further distinguishes between human and non-human objects and actions, and uses propriety to distinguish a pleasurable combination of the former, congruity a pleasurable combination of the latter.

15. Samuel Monk, *The Sublime* (Ann Arbor, 1960). See also R. S. Crane's review of *The Sublime* in *Philological Quarterly,* XV (April, 1936), 165–67.

16. Monk refers to this passage from *Elements of Criticism* as an example of the problem critics encountered when they attempted to change the metaphorical ("height of style") to the literal ("height"), p. 114.

17. Trans. H. Rackham, III, lvii–lvix, Loeb Classical Library (Cambridge, 1948), pp. 173–77.

18. "Sources of the Elocutionary Movement in England: 1700–1748," *The Quarterly Journal of Speech,* XLV (February, 1959), 1–18.

19. *Ibid.,* p. 8.

20. I am indebted to Professor G. P. Mohrman for calling my attention to Le Brun's book. Professor Mohrman has examined Kame's relation to the elocutionary movement as well as the movement in general in two recent articles: "Kames and Elocution," *Speech Monographs,* XXXII (June, 1965), 198–206; and "The Language of Nature and Elocutionary Theory," *The Quarterly Journal of Speech,* LII (April, 1966), 116–24.

21. T. S. Eliot uses this phrase in his essay "The Metaphysical Poets," *Selected Essays* (London, 1961), p. 288.

Chapter Four

1. Helen W. Randall, *op. cit.,* p. 23n.

2. The reader interested in the history of rhetoric during this period should consult two excellent sources: W. S. Howell, *Logic and Rhetoric in England, 1500–1700* (Princeton, 1956); and William Phillips Sandford, *English Theories of Public Address, 1530–1828* (Columbus, 1931).

3. Randall, *op. cit.,* pp. 44–45.

4. *Ibid.,* p. 45. See also a recent article by Vincent Bevilacqua, "Lord Kames's Theory of Rhetoric," *Speech Monographs,* XXX (November, 1963), 309–27, in which he argues that the rhetorical theory of Kames and others in this "school," like Campbell and Blair, differed from the traditional Ciceronian or Ramist rhetoric in its attention "to the composition and criticism of literary works" (314). I do not feel that this kind of hyperdistinction is necessary. Bevilacqua makes too much of Kames's emphasis on literary works. Actually Kames regarded the poetry and drama from which he drew his illustrations as performances to be judged according to the naturalness of their sound and sense.

5. William Flint Thrall, Addison Hibbard, and C. Hugh Holman, *A Handbook to Literature* (New York, 1960), p. 394.

6. See the excellent discussion of the development of logic and rhetoric in the introduction to W. S. Howell's *Logic and Rhetoric in England, 1500–1700.* My discussion of these developments follows the line suggested by Howell.

7. Quintilian has an extensive discussion of tropes and figures in *Institutio Oratoria:* Book VIII, Chapter 6; and Book IX, Chapters 1–3. Interested readers should also consult Richard Sherry's *Treatise of Schemes and Tropes* (1550) and *Figures of Grammar and Rhetoric* (1555).

8. In *Sketches of the History of Man* (1774) rhetoric is given the province of "grace, elegance, and force, in thought and expression,"

logic that of "justness and accuracy of thought" (Vol. II, p. 235). While Kames's friend Thomas Reid is responsible for the actual working out of the distinction, Professor Bevilacqua has argued cogently that the distinction was approved by Kames. See "Lord Kames's Theory of Rhetoric," p. 315n.

9. *The Philosophy of Rhetoric,* ed. Lloyd F. Bitzer (Carbondale, 1963), p. 293.

10. Thrall, Hibbard, and Holman, *op. cit.,* p. 483.

11. *Elements,* III, p. 122.

12. Perhaps the Latin phrase *figura verborum* will clarify the meaning of "figure of style." As Quintilian uses the phrase, it refers exclusively to the shape of a word. "Style" has a much more general meaning today.

13. Trans. Ingram Bywater, *The Student's Oxford Aristotle,* VI (New York, 1942), para. 7.

14. *Ibid.,* para. 5.

15. *Ibid.,* para. 8.

16. See Dryden's essay "Of Dramatic Poesy" where Lisideius points out how French drama has also striven to conform to the unities. Lisideius, of course, approves of such strictness. *Essays of John Dryden,* ed. W. P. Ker, I (New York, 1961), 56–67.

17. "Of the Standard of Taste," *Essays Moral, Political, and Literary,* ed. T. H. Green and T. H. Grose, I (London, 1882), 266-84.

18. "Kames and the Anthropological Approach to Criticism," *op. cit.,* p. 229.

19. This useful phrase appears in an article dealing with Kames from which Horn quotes: Wilhelm Dilthey, "Die drei Epochen der modernen Asthetik und ihre heutige Aufgabe," *Gesammelte Schriften,* VI (Leipzig-Berlin, 1924), esp. pp. 258–60.

20. Horn, *op. cit.,* p. 229.

Chapter Five

1. *Sketches of the History of Man,* I (Edinburgh, 1774), v. All subsequent references to *Sketches* will be to this edition and will be indicated in the text.

2. *The Art of History* (New York, 1926), p. 14. Quoted in William C. Lehmann, *John Millar of Glasgow* (Cambridge, 1960), p. 101.

3. J. B. Bury develops the relation between the ancient/modern controversy and the ideas of primitivism and progress in his book *The Idea of Progress* (New York, 1932). Lois Whitney, curiously enough, does not make this relationship in *Primitivism and the Idea of Progress* (Baltimore, 1934).

4. Ross, *op. cit.,* pp. 236–38.

5. See Chapter IX, "Attempts at Compromise," in Lois Whitney's *Primitivism and the Idea of Progress,* pp. 277–89.

6. A. O. Lovejoy, "Monboddo and Rousseau," *Essays in the History of Ideas,* pp. 41–42. All quotes in the preceding two paragraphs are from these pages of Lovejoy's essay.

7. The phrase is Ian Ross's, *op. cit.,* p. 236.

8. Lois Whitney comments that Kames's solution to the contradiction between Scripture and historical theory was only half-hearted, "for when he comes to discuss the tribes of American Indians he forgets all about it and argues for separate creation," *op. cit.,* p. 279n.

9. *Essays, op. cit.,* p. 136.

10. Quoted from Kames in Whitney, *op. cit.,* pp. 98–99.

11. *Sketches,* II, 153–64 (1788 ed.). Quoted in Whitney, pp. 277–78.

Chapter Six

1. *The Poems of Ossian,* trans. James Macpherson (Edinburgh, 1926), p. ix.

2. My source for these details, unless otherwise noted, has been the *Report of the Committee of the Highland Society of Scotland Appointed to Inquire into the Nature and Authenticity of the Poems of Ossian* (Edinburgh, 1805).

3. *Report,* p. 28.

4. *The Works of Thomas Gray,* ed. Gosse, III (London, 1884), 65. Quoted in J. S. Smart, *James Macpherson* (London, 1905), p. 131n.

5. *The Yale Edition of Horace Walpole's Correspondence,* ed. W. S. Lewis, VIII, (New Haven, 1939), 407. Quoted in Smart, p. 136.

6. Smart, p. 136.

7. G. M. Fraser called this "One of the most eloquent and convincing pronouncements on the wrong side of a case that can be found in English literary history." "The Truth About Macpherson's 'Ossian'," *Quarterly Review* CCXLV (1925), 331.

8. *The Letters of David Hume,* ed. J. Y. T. Greig, I (Oxford, 1932), pp. 398–400.

9. *Boswell's Life of Johnson,* ed. G. B. Hill, rev. L. F. Powell, I (Oxford, 1934), pp. 261–63.

10. *Ibid.,* II, 297-98, n.2.

11. *Report,* p. 152.

12. See Derick S. Thomson, *The Gaelic Sources of Macpherson's "Ossian"* (Edinburgh, 1951), pp. 1–12, 73–81.

13. Donald Foerster, "Mid-Eighteenth-Century Scotch Criticism of Homer," *Studies in Philology,* XL (1943), 425–46; "Scottish Primitivism

and the Historical Approach," *Philological Quarterly*, XXIX (1950), 307–23. See also Foerster's *Homer in English Criticism* (New Haven, 1947).

14. Foerster, "Mid-Eighteenth-Century Scotch Criticism of Homer," *op. cit.*, p. 445.

15. *Sketches*, I, 282–83. Later scholars have disputed Kames's assertion that there are no anachronisms in the Ossian poems. One notes anachronisms in both architecture and weaponry: "The Caledonian princes are lodged in massive structures of stone. When Balclutha was destroyed, a river was removed from its bed by the fall of the ruins. It has halls in which the fire resounded, towers and courts. In short, it was a feudal castle, removed to an age where it was out of place: the Kings of Ireland lived in houses of wood surrounded by earthen ramparts. . . . Another anachronism is the use of the bow and arrow by armies in battle, which we find everywhere in *Ossian*. Although a primitive weapon, the bow was not often employed by the Celts of the heroic age." J. S. Smart, *op. cit.*, pp. 125–26.

16. Foerster, *op. cit.*, p. 425.

17. "English Neo-Classical Criticism: An Outline Sketch," *Critics and Criticism* (Chicago, 1952), pp. 372–88.

Selected Bibliography

PRIMARY SOURCES

Dictionary of Decisions. Edinburgh: R. Watkins, A. Kinkaid, 1741.

Elements of Criticism. 2nd ed. 3 vols. Edinburgh: A. Kinkaid and J. Bell, 1763. First edition published in Edinburgh in 1762.

Elucidations respecting the Common and Statute Law of Scotland. Edinburgh: W. Creech, 1777.

Essays on the Principles of Morality and Natural Religion. Edinburgh: A. Kinkaid and A. Donaldson, 1751.

Essays upon several Subjects concerning British Antiquities. Edinburgh: A. Kinkaid, 1747.

Essays upon several Subjects in Law. Edinburgh: A. Kinkaid, 1732.

The Gentleman Farmer. Edinburgh: W. Creech, 1776.

Historical Law Tracts. Edinburgh: A. Millar, A. Kinkaid, and J. Bell, 1758.

Introduction to the Art of Thinking. Edinburgh: A. Kinkaid and J. Bell, 1761.

Loose Hints upon Education. Edinburgh: J. Bell, 1781.

Principles of Equity. Edinburgh: A. Millar, A. Kinkaid, and J. Bell, 1760.

Progress of Flax-husbandry in Scotland. Edinburgh: Sands, Murray, and Cochran, 1766.

Remarkable Decisions of the Court of Session 1716–1728. Edinburgh: T. Ruddiman, 1728.

Remarkable Decisions of the Court of Session, 1730–1752. Edinburgh: A. Kinkaid and J. Bell, 1766.

Select Decisions of the Court Session, 1752–1768. Edinburgh: J. Bell, 1780.

Sketches of the History of Man. Edinburgh: W. Creech, 1774.

Statute Laws of Scotland. Edinburgh: A. Kinkaid and A. Donaldson, 1757.

SECONDARY SOURCES

1. General Criticism

BATE, WALTER JACKSON. *From Classic to Romantic: Premises of Taste in Eighteenth-Century England.* New York: Harper and Brothers, 1961. A paperback reprint of Bate's pioneering study of eighteenth-century esthetics; includes chapters on associationism and sympathy.

BURY, J. B. *The Idea of Progress.* New York: Dover, 1932. Standard work on this subject.

CASSIRER, ERNST. *The Philosophy of the Enlightenment.* Princeton: Princeton University Press, 1951. Has a larger scope than does Leslie Stephen, but is in many ways a clearer discussion of eighteenth-century intellectual background.

CRANE, R. S. "English Neo-Classical Criticism: An Outline Sketch," *Critics and Criticism.* Chicago: University of Chicago Press, 1952. Precise, extremely useful categories of critics and critical theories.

DAICHES, DAVID. *The Paradox of Scottish Culture: The Eighteenth-Century Experience.* London; Oxford University Press, 1964. Brief but excellent introduction to eighteenth-century Scottish thought.

HANZO, THOMAS A. "Lattitude and Restoration Criticism," *Anglistica,* Vol. XII. Copenhagen: Rosenkilde and Bagger, 1961. First chapter, "The Argument for Latitude," an indispensable introduction to late seventeenth-century history of ideas, especially to rationalism and neo-Platonism.

HIPPLE, WALTER J. *The Beautiful, the Sublime, and the Picturesque in Eighteenth-Century British Aesthetic Theory.* Carbondale: The Southern Illinois University Press, 1957. Attempt to systematize the critical theories of the major eighteenth-century critics. Tends to see unity and consistency where none exists. Has a chapter on Lord Kames.

HOWELL, WILBUR S. *Logic and Rhetoric in England, 1500–1700.* Princeton: Princeton University Press, 1956. Thorough examination of developments in the history of rhetoric.

———. "Sources of the Elocutionary Movement in England: 1700–1748," *The Quarterly Journal of Speech,* XLV (February, 1959), 1–18. Continuation of Howell's book. Suggests directions he will take in another book.

LEHMANN, WILLIAM C. *John Millar of Glasgow.* Cambridge: Cambridge University Press, 1960. Important chapter on eighteenth-century Scottish thought.

Selected Bibliography

LOVEJOY, A. O. *Essays in the History of Ideas.* New York: G. P. Putnam's Sons, 1960. Lucid exposition of such crucial eighteenth-
century ideas as nature, Deism, classicism, and primitivism.

McCOSH, JAMES. *The Scottish Philosophy, from Hutcheson to Balfour.*
New York: R. Carter and Brothers, 1875.

McKENZIE, GORDON. *Critical Responsiveness: A Study of the Psychological Current in Later Eighteenth-Century Criticism.* Berkeley
and Los Angeles: University of California Press, 1949. Comple-
ments Walter Hipple's book. Organized according to ideas in critical theory, such as taste, association, figurative language, and imagination. Spends a good deal of space on Kames.

MONK, SAMUEL. *The Sublime.* Ann Arbor: University of Michigan
Press, 1960. Reprint of an important early study of the changes in a
critical idea in the course of the eighteenth century.

MOSSNER, ERNEST C. *The Life of David Hume.* London: Thomas Nel-
son, 1954. Definitive biography of Hume and the best introduction to the Scottish cultural milieu available.

STEPHEN, LESLIE. *English Thought in the Eighteenth Century.* 2 vols.
London: Rupert Hart-Davis, 1962. Basic work for an understand-
ing of the philosophical and moral background of the English
Enlightenment.

WELLEK, RENÉ. *A History of Modern Criticism.* Vol. I. New Haven:
Yale University Press, 1955. Chapter 6 deals with eighteenth-century Scottish criticism.

WHITNEY, LOIS. *Primitivism and the Idea of Progress.* Baltimore:
The Johns Hopkins Press, 1934. Good study of the relationships
between these two ideas, but lacks the comprehensiveness and insights of Bury's book.

WILLEY, BASIL. *The Eighteenth-Century Background.* London: Chatto
and Windus, 1940. Important essays on concept of nature, on Deism, and on natural morality in the period.

2. Biography and Criticism

BEVILACQUA, VINCENT. "Lord Kames's Theory of Rhetoric," *Speech
Monographs,* XXX (November, 1963), 309–27. Brief and generally sound summary of Kames's ideas. Perhaps a bit weak on the
philosophical background of the period.

———. "Rhetoric and Human Nature in Kames's *Elements of Criticism,*" *The Quarterly Journal of Speech,* XLVIII (1962), 46–50.
Handling of the critical problems really too brief to be very useful.

———. "The Rhetorical Theory of Henry Home, Lord Kames." Unpublished doctoral dissertation, University of Illinois, 1961. At-

tempts to put the ideas in *Elements* into traditional rhetorical categories. Generally unsuccessful. Professor Bevilacqua has modified his ideas substantially in later articles.

BOSWELL, JAMES. "Materials for Writing the Life of Lord Kames," *Private Papers from Malahide Castle.* Ed. Geoffrey Scott and Frederick Pottle. Vol. XV (Mount Vernon, New York: W. E. Rudge, 1928–1934), 260–316. The result of Boswell's interviews with Kames from 1778 to 1782. The most reliable of the early biographical studies of Kames.

BUNDY, MURRAY W. "Lord Kames and the Maggots in Amber," *Journal of English and Germanic Philology,* XLV (April, 1946), 199–208. A highly critical review of Helen Randall's book on Lord Kames. Bundy's acerbic remarks sound a bit like those of Samuel Johnson and have about as much relevance to the Scottish literary scene.

FOERSTER, DONALD. "Mid-Eighteenth-Century Scotch Criticism of Homer," *Studies in Philology,* XL (1943), 425–46.

———. "Scottish Primitivism and the Historical Approach," *Philological Quarterly,* XXIX (1950), 307–23. Makes distinctions between historicism and esthetics which are unwarranted.

HORN, ANDRÁS. "Kames and the Anthropological Approach to Criticism," *Philological Quarterly,* XLIV (April, 1965), 211–233. The best study of Kames's critical theory yet to appear.

HUME, DAVID. *New Letters of David Hume.* Ed. Raymond Klibansky and Ernest C. Mossner. Oxford: Oxford University Press, 1954. Contains some previously unpublished letters from Hume to Kames that reveal their close relationship.

———. "Of the Standard of Taste," *Essays Moral, Political, and Literary.* Ed. T. H. Green and T. H. Grose. Vol. I. London: Longmans, Green, 1882. Contains several parallels to Kames's essay on the same subject, suggesting a possible influence of Kames's thought on Hume.

McKENZIE, GORDON. "Lord Kames and the Mechanist Tradition," *Essays and Studies, University of California Publications in English,* XIV (1943), 93–121. Perhaps, like Helen Randall, a bit too insistent on Kames's empiricism.

RANDALL, HELEN W. "The Critical Theory of Lord Kames," *Smith College Studies in Languages and Literature,* XXII (1940–41), Nos. 1–4. A pioneer study of Kames. Contains the most extensive biography published to date. Concentrates on *Elements of Criticism.* Based a bit too inflexibly on thesis that the structure of the book is Newtonian analysis and synthesis.

Selected Bibliography

ROSS, IAN S. "Boswell in Search of a Father? or a Subject?" *A Review of English Literature,* V, i (1964), 19–34. Chapter V of Ross's University of Texas dissertation. Considers the relationship between Boswell and Lord Kames.

—————. "A Bluestocking over the Border: Mrs. Elizabeth Montagu's Aesthetic Adventures in Scotland, 1766," *Huntington Library Quarterly,* XXVIII (1965), 213–33. Kames entertained Mrs. Montagu and began a rather extensive correspondence with her subsequent to this visit.

—————" 'The Most Arrogant Man in the World': The Life and Writings of Henry Home, Lord Kames." Unpublished doctoral dissertation, University of Texas (1960). This is an excellent biographical study of Kames, and Professor Ross has spent the last several years doing further research on Kames's life and times. His forthcoming book should be a definitive biography.

—————. "Scots Law and Scots Criticism: The Case of Lord Kames," *Philological Quarterly,* XLV (1966), 614–23. Brings together two of Kames's chief preoccupations.

Index